HISTORIC JOURNAL

CENTRAL RAILROAD OF NEW JERSEY

STATIONS, STRUCTURES, & MARINE EQUIPMENT

Benjamin L. Bernhart

edited by Jay Leinbach
and Dr. John H.L. Bernhart

photographic contributors:
National Archives, William Krug
and James D. Brownback

ISBN #1-891402-07-2

In June, 2004, Benjamin Bernhart rode the Reading Railroad passenger
coach at the North Carolina Railroad Museum with his sons,
Nicollas (3 years) and Brenden (7 months).

Dedicated to
Brenden James Bernhart,
the newest addition to the Bernhart family.
May he grow up to be a railfan like his father.

**Brenden James Bernhart was named in honor of James D. Brownback,
a former employee of the Reading Company and the Philadelphia,
Reading and Pottsville Telegraph Company (PRPT Co.).
James Brownback is the current owner of the PRPT Co.**

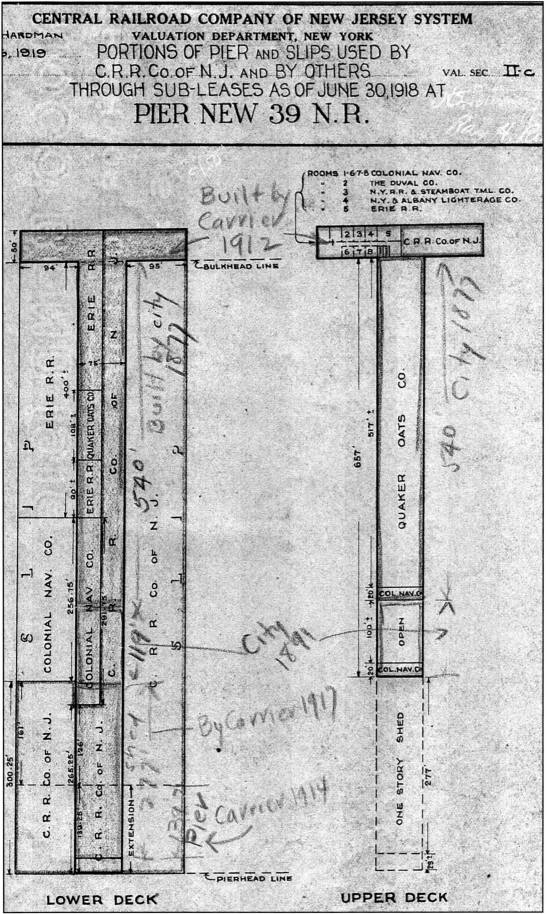

CENTRAL RAILROAD COMPANY OF NEW JERSEY SYSTEM

HARDMAN   VALUATION DEPARTMENT, NEW YORK
6, 1919   PORTIONS OF PIER AND SLIPS USED BY
C.R.R.Co.OF N.J. AND BY OTHERS   VAL. SEC. II-c
THROUGH SUB-LEASES AS OF JUNE 30, 1918 AT

PIER NEW 39 N.R.

ROOMS 1-6-7-8 COLONIAL NAV. CO.
" 2 THE DUVAL CO.
" 3 N.Y. R.R. & STEAMBOAT T.ML. CO.
" 4 N.Y. & ALBANY LIGHTERAGE CO.
" 5 ERIE R.R.

Built by Carrier 1912

Built by city 1877

By Carrier 1917

Pier Carrier 1914

City 1891

LOWER DECK   UPPER DECK

Above -- A diagram of Pier 39 shows the different sections of the pier that were leased and sublet.

There is conflicting information on the exact year that Pier 39 was constructed. According to a lease agreement dated March 26, 1907, the CNJ leased the entire pier from the City of New York. The lease states that the pier was constructed in 1877 by the city. However, Interstate Commerce Commission records state that the Pier was built in 1910 - 1911 which may be a rebuilt date.

In 1914 the CNJ enlarged the pier by adding a section 45' wide x 132' long. It was once again enlarged by the CNJ in 1917 with the addition of a 69' wide x 277' long section. This extension brought the entire length of the pier to 963 feet.

On August 8, 1907, the CNJ sublet the northerly half of the pier and bulkhead shed to the Manhattan Terminal Company, which in turn sublet the northern half of the lower level to the Manhattan Navigation Company. The Manhattan Navigation Company then sublet space to the Erie Railroad and a mooring berth to the Colonial Navigation Company.

In 1908 the Manhattan Terminal Company sublet additional space to the Colonial Navigation Company, the Duval Company, and the New York Railroad & Steamboat Terminal Company. The Manhattan Terminal Company paid $28,750 per year for the first ten years of the lease and then $31,625 per year for the remaining 10 years of its lease.

In 1944 the CNJ transferred the lease of Pier 39 to the Baltimore & Ohio Railroad.

Top -- In 1904 the CNJ leased Pier 46 at W. 10th Street. The CNJ operated a freight station at this location. In the photograph the bulkhead shed as well as the freight station building can be seen. The operation of the freight station was discontinued in 1945.

Middle / Left -- Pier 46 looking towards the Hudson River.

Bottom -- Between 1905 and 1941 the CNJ leased space at Pier 81 at West 41st Street for use by the Sandy Hook Route. The Hudson River Day Line shared the space with the CNJ.

Middle / Right -- Two views of Pier 80 at West 40th Street.

Above -- A 25-ton stationary electric crane at the Bronx Terminal.

On August 16, 1907, the CNJ opened the Bronx Terminal along the Harlem River. The terminal was located at a convenient location to serve the boroughs of Bronx, Brooklyn, upper Manhattan, and Long Island. Before the opening of this terminal the CNJ used the Erie Railroad Bronx Terminal until they were evicted in 1905. When the Bronx Terminal opened it consisted of a circular freight house which had a platform space of 40' x 100'. There were 17 tracks with a capacity of 73 cars, of which 56 afford team track delivery. The yard was also equipped with one float bridge, one 25-ton electric traveling crane covering 15 cars for loading and unloading, one 25 ton stationary electric crane covering 2 cars for loading and unloading, one 1-ton gasoline operated magnet crane used for handling scrap iron and similar commodities, one ramp with a 50 ton capacity, and one wagon scale.

In 1925 the CNJ purchased oil-electric locomotive #1000 to replace steam locomotives to drill cars. Number 1000 was the first of this type of locomotive manufactured in the United States for railroad transportation.

On March 15, 1927 a new yard of 10 tracks was added to the Bronx Terminal. This new yard was connected to the terminal by running a single track under the Third Avenue Bridge. The new yard provided space for an additional 94 cars, of which 36 afforded team track delivery.

Throughout the 1930's the terminal averaged 800 tons daily or 20,000 tons monthly. Cars were received and forwarded by car floats to and from Jersey City via the Harlem, East, and Hudson Rivers.

The Bronx Terminal closed in 1962.

Top -- The engine house at the Bronx Terminal.
Middle and Bottom -- Two different views of the Bronx Terminal, circa 1938. From the Collection of James D. Brownback.

CHAPTER 2
MARINE EQUIPMENT

Sandy Hook Ferries

Passenger boat service operated between New York City and (depending on the era) Port Monmouth, Sandy Hook or Atlantic Highlands, where train connections could be made to nearly all New Jersey points. On January 13, 1860, the *S.S. Alice Price* made the first trip from New York City to Port Monmouth, connecting with the Raritan and Delaware Bay Railroad. That night a strong storm hit Port Monmouth tearing away the outer portion of the Port Monmouth dock. Until repairs could be made the *Alice Price* could only dock at high tide.

After a period of operating to Port Monmouth, a new dock was constructed at Sandy Hook. However, Sandy Hook was a government reservation and a testing ground for artillery. In 1892 this dock was abandoned and service terminated at Atlantic Highlands Pier.

The Sandy Hook steamers that were used during the history of this line included: *Charles J. Osborn, Fall River, Jesse Hoyt, Josephine, Long Branch, Plymouth Rock, Taminend, Thomas Collyer, Americus, Antelope, Aurora, Cape Charles, City of Richmond, Crystal Wave, Day Star, Jane Mosseley, John Sylvester, Keyport, Magenta, Meta, Metropolis, Naushon, Nelley White, Neversink, Newport, Rip Van Winkle, River Belle, River Queen, T.V. Arrowsmith, William Cook, William Harrison, Wyoming, Alice Price, The Empire State, St.Johns, Kill Von Kull, Chancellor, Asbury Park, Monmouth,* and *Sandy Hook.* Some of these steamers were also used on excursions.

ASBURY PARK

SANDY HOOK

KILL VON KULL

Built by James Simonson and the Novelty Iron Works in 1857, the boat was used primarily for the hauling of freight and cattle. During the early stages of the Civil War, the boat was used to haul troops to Annapolis. In 1879-1880 the boat was rebuilt into a passenger vessel at a cost of $125,000. On March 3, 1889 the *Kill Von Kull* burned at Elizabethport.

SANDY HOOK BOATS— THEN AND NOW

The S. S. Monmouth approaching Atlantic Highlands, N. J.

The old S. S. Elizabeth, built along the lines of a ferry-boat.

Passengers boarding the S. S. Sandy Hook at New York City

Sleek and fast in its day—the S. S. St. Johns

Another boat used early in the Sandy Hook service—the Kill von Kull.

The S.S. Longbranch which carried many famous people.

Another echo of the past—the S. S. Empire State.

The modern S.S. Sandy Hook approaching New York City.

Above -- A Page from the June, 1936, *Reading - Jersey Central Magazine* depicting the steamers that served the Sandy Hook route. Note that the *Elizabeth* is depicted. The *Elizabeth* spent most of its career as a ferry between Jersey City and New York City. Collection of James D. Brownback.

CENTRAL

By mid-June 1864, the *Central* was completed. It had a lower deck size of 225' x 65' x 13'3" and an upper deck size of 178' x 63' x 14'. The ship had a 217' keel and weighed 1,023 tons. The engine was built by Washington Iron Works in Newburgh, New York. The *Central* and the *Communipaw* began their careers by opening the Liberty Street route on July 29, 1864. The *Central* was under the command of Captain Charles A. Woolsey. The ferry was condemned in May, 1882, and was scheduled to be scraped. However, in September, 1882, she was rebuilt. In 1883, the Edison Electric Company installed electric lights on-board and in the fall of 1891 the ship once again received a complete overhaul with new boilers, engine, stack, paint, and upgraded electric lights. In 1892 the ferry was painted dark green, which remained the standard color until 1952. The *Central* was retired in September, 1902, and was taken to a scrap yard in Perth Amboy.

COMMUNIPAW

The *Communipaw* was built to the same specifications as the *Central*. In 1892 the ferry was painted the standard dark green from the cream color that it had been painted in June, 1884. The *Communipaw* was retired in March, 1903.

ELIZABETH

On November 15, 1866, the *Elizabeth* was launched from Bergen Point. The ship weighed 1,079 tons and had a 215' keel. The *Elizabeth* was 2' wider then the *Central* and *Communipaw*. In 1892 the ferry was painted dark green from the cream color that it had been painted in August, 1884. On October 22, 1901, the *Elizabeth* suffered severe fire damage when fire broke out as it neared Jersey City. The 12 passengers aboard were unaware of the fire and departed from the ferry as normal. A Lehigh Valley Railroad tug tried to put out the fire, but the *Elizabeth* was towed from the slip and beached on the Communipaw flats.

PLAINFIELD

The *Plainfield* was launched on July 25, 1868. The ferry had a 213' keel and weighed 1,092 tons. On June 3, 1869, the *Plainfield* made its first revenue run with 300 guests, including the mayor of Plainfield, New Jersey. In the spring of 1892 the ferry received an extensive overhaul. Replacing pea green paint from July, 1887, the *Plainfield* was painted dark green in 1892. The *Plainfield* was retired prior to May, 1903.

FANWOOD

Weighing 1,092 tons, the *Fanwood* was built in 1876 with a 213' keel. Fletcher, Harrison & Company built the engine with a (53' x 12' cylinder.) The *Fanwood* was first used to establish service to Clarkson Street beginning on July 17, 1876. This route was discontinued on May 10, 1877. In 1883 the Edison Electric Company installed electric lights on-board the *Fanwood*, making this ferry the first of the CNJ ferries to have electric lighting. In the spring of 1892 the ship received a complete overhaul with new boilers, engine, stack, paint, and upgraded electric lights. In 1892 she was painted dark green. On March 19, 1904, *Fanwood* was towed to Perth Amboy and then to the J.H. Gregory scrap yard.

EASTON

Built with a steel hull, the *Easton* was completed in 1893. The ship had 7' diameter propellers. The lower deck was 100' long with the upper deck having a length of 80'. Between 1893-1897 the *Easton* was chartered until the Whitehall Street slips became available. Riverside & Fort Lee Ferry Company purchased the *Easton* on February 19, 1906. The upper cabin was removed and the ship was renamed *Leonia*. It was scrapped in 1948.

MAUCH CHUNK

The Mauch Chunk was built under the same specifications as the *Easton*. Like the *Easton*, the *Mauch Chunk* was chartered from 1893-1897. Approaching the Whitehall Street slips on October 14, 1901, the *Mauch Chunk*, piloted by Captain S.C. Griffin, collided with Staten Island ferry the *Northfield*, piloted by Captain Abraham Johnson. The *Northfield* was 3/4 out of the slip when the *Mauch Chunk* rammed into her. The *Mauch Chunk* received only minor damage, but punctured the hull of the *Northfield*. The *Mauch Chunk* unloaded and reloaded to continue its trip back to Jersey City. Meanwhile, the *Northfield* drifted up the East River and sank up to its upper deck when it touched East River Pier 9. The *Northfield* was hauling nearly 1,000 passengers, of which 5 drowned. Both Captains received a 30 day suspension. The *Mauch Chunk* was repaired in October of 1901. On February 26, 1906, she was sold to Philadelphia & Kaighn's Point Ferry Company for $46,500. In 1922 it was renamed *Margate* and was again renamed *Mount Hood* in 1927.

LAKEWOOD

In February 1900, a set of three identical ferries were ordered from Harlan & Hollingsworth. The boats weighed 1,106 tons each. The *Lakewood* was delivered on August 9, 1901. On January 17, 1950, the *Lakewood* was burned at the Jersey City marine repair yard. She was then rebuilt with a steel superstructure at the Bethlehem Steel shipyard at Mariners Harbor. When she reentered service on April 19, 1951, she bore the name *Elizabeth*.

BOUND BROOK

Built to the same specifications as the *Lakewood* and *Red Bank*, the *Bound Brook* was delivered in December, 1901. During a hurricane on September 14, 1944 the *Bound Brook* broke loose and grounded herself on Bedloes Island. She was stuck there for 30 days.

RED BANK

This was the last of the "triplets" to be delivered. After a lengthy legal battle, the CNJ was ordered to stop operating to and using the Whitehall Street slips. The *Red Bank* made the last run to this location on June 24, 1905. The following day the *Red Bank* made the first revenue trip to the new 23rd Street ferry terminal, which was still under construction. In April, 1963, the *Red Bank* was stripped of parts and retired.

PLAINFIELD

Above -- The second *Plainfield* was launched in May, 1904, and was retired in 1954. She was sold in September of 1955.

ELIZABETH

Built by Harlan & Hollingsworth, the *Elizabeth* was part of a four identical ferry order placed in 1903. The ferry weighed 1,197 tons. Her sister ships were the *Wilkes-Barre*, *Somerville* and *Cranford*. CNJ president Mr. Besler attended the launching party of *Elizabeth* which was held on August 11, 1904. The ferry was delivered to Jersey City on November 7, 1904.

WILKES-BARRE

In December, 1904, the *Wilkes-Barre* was delivered and placed on the Whitehall Street run. It was sold to Dr. H. R. Axelrod for $16,500 on July 26, 1966. She was then towed to Exchange Place.

SOMERVILLE

The *Somerville* was the last of the "quads" to arrive from Harlan & Hollingsworth in March, 1906. She began her career on the 23rd Street route. The CNJ applied to the Interstate Commerce Commission on September 18, 1941 for abandonment of the 23rd Street route and on October 2, 1941, the approval was given. In 1926, the average passenger count was 47 with 10 vehicles per trip, compared to the 1940 average of 38 passengers and 7 vehicles. This was a lose of 210,000 passengers and 53,000 vehicles. The *Somerville* was the last CNJ ferry to leave the 23rd Street terminal on November 14, 1941, at 9:53 PM. Mr. P. Lavender of Jersey City purchased the last ticket. The *Somerville* was forced to go out of service in November of 1964 when it failed it inspection and in February, 1965, the *Somerville* was sold to Ellis Marine Corp.

CRANFORD

In late December, 1905, the *Cranford* arrived and was placed on the 23rd Street route. On March 19, 1965, the *Cranford* was retired and sold to George Mauro for $3,250 for use as a restaurant at Brielle, New Jersey.

WESTFIELD

The *Westfield* was delivered on June 3, 1911 and was retired in 1954. She was sold in September of 1955.

ELIZABETH

Rebuilt from parts of the *Lakewood*, the *Elizabeth* reentered service on April 19, 1951. This was the third ship in the fleet to be honored with the name *Elizabeth*. She made her last run in April, 1967. Upon arriving at Jersey City, she was stripped by souvenir hunters. In July, 1967, the *Elizabeth* was sold to the Mowbray Tug & Barge Company for $26,500. She currently resides near the Benjamin Franklin Bridge in Philadelphia. She was docked at that location to be used as a Hooters Restaurant. She is currently in poor condition and is listing to one side.

Tug Boats

BRIDGETON

BLUE RIDGE

MANAGER

JERSEY CENTRAL

NEWARK

BETHLEHEM

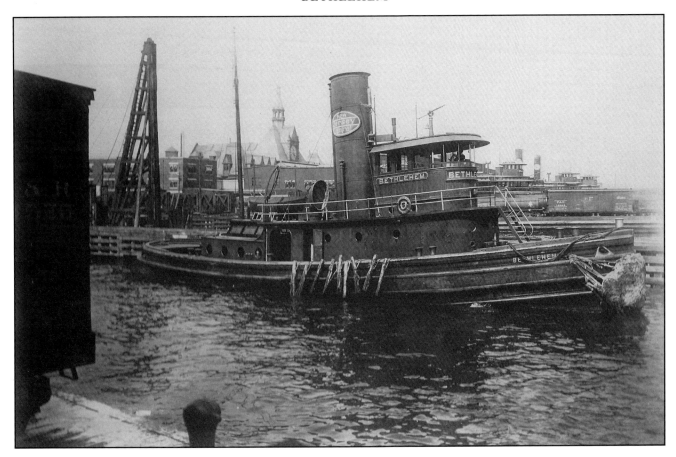

SEA BRIGHT

WHITE ASH

KEYPORT

Lighter Service Equipment

Lighterage service began in New York Harbor around 1840. The boats used were sail lighters without keels. This type of ship was used until the mid 1860s when the open deck scow, the hand winch scow, the covered barge and the hoisting lighter began to be used. Later the steam lighter, a self-navigable boat, was introduced to this service.

Lighterage service provided a means to move freight from Jersey City to NYC. The CNJ maintained two large covered docks and two open docks in Jersey City to facilitate this trade. During 1936 it was not uncommon for the lighterage deparment of the CNJ to handle over 1000 cars of freight at Jersey City at one time. During the apple season of 1935 - 1936 the CNJ delivered 1207 cars of apples, by means of lighters, to New York City.

Derrick Lighter #400
Derrick Lighter #400 with tug boat *Blue Ridge*.

Derrick Lighter #404

Derrick Lighter #401

Hoist Lighter #110

Hoist Lighter #104

Hoist Lighter #111

Hoist Lighter #113

Hoist Lighter #130

Hoist Lighter #115

Hoist Lighter #221

Hoist Lighter #226

Hoist Lighter #209

Covered Barge #302

Covered Barge #300

Covered Barge #304

Covered Barge #316

Top and Middle -- Loaded car floats at Bronx Terminal float bridge, circa 1938. Collection of James D. Brownback.

Bottom -- Jersey Central Tug *Belmar* moving barges across the Hudson River, circa 1936. Collection of James D. Brownback.

Shop Pantoon *"Spunky Sally"* with *SOMERVILLE, BOUND BROOK, MONMOUTH* and **Car Float #34**

Pile Driver #1

CHAPTER 3
JERSEY CITY TERMINAL COMPLEX

The Jersey City Terminal complex was built on land and marsh land was known as Communipaw Cove. This site was first used by the Dutch settlement of New Netherland in 1661 as the terminal for the first ferry service across the Hudson River to Manhattan. The Central Railroad of New Jersey began to develop this area in 1860. In 1860 the New Jersey legislature granted permission for a rail line to be constructed over the Newark Bay from Elizabethport to Communipaw Avenue. Opening for passenger service in 1864, this line proved to be profitable. That same year a station with a temporary ferry slip and an open platform were constructed in Jersey City. This sparked the beginning of the Jersey City Terminal complex, which would one day stretch over a mile and half along the water-front.

Work began in 1864 for a permanent headhouse (station) and two ferry slips at Jersey City. To construct their facilities on the marshland of the cove, the Central Railroad of New Jersey purchased large amounts of garbage from New York City. Not only were the mud flats filled in with garbage, but the railroad filled in some 4,000 feet into the Hudson River. One can only image the smell of rotting garbage drifting into downtown Jersey City. In 1875 the station was enlarged to handle the ever growing number of trains and passengers it handled. On July 4, 1879 this station served 105 westbound and 97 trains eastbound.

With the dedication of the Statue of Liberty in 1886, Jersey City became known as the "Gateway to the West." Capitalizing on this notion, the Central Railroad of New Jersey adopted the Statue of Liberty as part of the railroad's logo. The railroad also realized that the present station and facilities would not be sufficient for future traffic. Plans were quickly drawn up for a new terminal. During the week of June 28, 1889, the new station was opened for business. The new commodious brick station was built by Peabody & Stearns of Boston in Victorian style. By 1892 the station was serving, on average, 153 trains westbound and 152 trains eastbound. In 1899 a large electric sign was added on the river side of the station.

Between 1912 and 1915 the entire station and ferry slips were completely rebuilt and modernized. Work began on this overhaul in May, 1912, with the construction of two temporary ferry slips, one on each side of the old ferry station. The new ferry house was a two story building which housed four slips with double deck loading capacity. The upper concourse was 50' x 302' while the lower vehicle concourse was 75' x 348'. The hand operated ferry bridges were replaced with modern electric ones. The ferry station was torn down after the discontinuance of ferry service from this terminal.

The 1889 station building was kept but was completely remodeled. The most noticeable change was the creation of a new waiting room created from old office space on the north side of the main room. The 1889 train sheds were torn down between April 22 and May 12, 1913, with the use of a travelling crane that was constructed out of three old signal bridges. The new Bush-type concrete and steel train shed was constructed from south to north allowing for a minimum of at least 15 tracks available at any given time. The new train shed became the largest Bush-type ever constructed. It covered 20 tracks and could hold 232 passengers cars compared to the mere 84 of the one it replaced. The train shed was 390' wide, 817' long over tracks 1-17, 676' long over tracks 18-20 and contained 16-20' wide platforms. In 1914, on the average, the new station complex handled 54,000 passengers and 400 trains each day.

In December, 1966, the state of New Jersey purchased the station complex and 49.5 acres of land for $1,600,000 and incorporated it as part of Liberty State Park.

This unique photograph of the interior of the outside waiting room was taken at 9:55 AM during the holiday shopping season of 1937, a time when the waiting room is bustling with activity. This photograph was taken by a railroad photographer by using a long exposure time. By using a very long exposure the camera does not register the countless people in the waiting room due to the fact that they are in motion. The camera only captures objects that are still. Collection of James D. Brownback.

Top and Bottom -- Two photographs taken around 1916 depict an overview of the Jersey City Terminal Complex. The following buildings are labled in the photographs: ferry house, passenger station headhouse, post office building, train concourse, express building and freight station. The express building was built in 1912 and was a three-story 45'x710' brick and concrete structure. The post office building was built in 1915 and was a three story 52'x136' brick structure.

Page 28 & 29 -- Bird's-eye view of Jersey City Terminal Complex, circa 1938. Collection of James D. Brownback.

BIRD'S-EYE VIEW OF THE C. R. R. OF N. J.
TERMINAL, JERSEY CITY, N. J.

Top and Middle / Left -- Two views of the Jersey City ferry slips and station as seen from a ferry. The Victorian style clock tower of the station headhouse can be seen in the background.

Middle / Right -- Freight crane at Jersey Avenue.

Bottom -- The freight house was located south of the station headhouse. The post office building was located between the freight house and the station.

Top -- Tinsmith storeroom. The freight house can be seen to the right of the storeroom. An old box car body was placed behind the tinsmith storeroom to supply additional storage.

Middle / Top -- The carpenter shop and cement storage was located at Jersey Avenue. The use of old box car and old passenger car bodies for addition storage or office space was quite common, as seen in this photograph and the one above.

Middle / Bottom -- The watchman with his faithful campanion posed for the ICC valuation photographer at Johnston Avenue. The building to the left of the watchbox was used for storage.

Page 32 / Top -- In 1914 the Central Railroad of New Jersey built several new brick and tile buildings near Johnston Avenue. They included a tile two-story passenger car repair rest house which was 28' x 122', a tile two story 34' x 144' building used by Pullman, a tile two-story storehouse, and a brick two-story 50' x 187' service building. The service building took power from the Communipaw power house and transformed it. The service building also provided steam heat to the terminal complex.

Bottom -- The passenger repair service buildings were located on the south side of Johnston Avenue.

Middle -- Float bridge #5 was originally built in 1907 and was rebuilt in 1924. It was replaced in 1943. Float bridge #5 was towed to the Baltimore & Ohio Railroad at St. George to replace one that had burned. In 1958 float bridge #5 was replaced once again with a new float bridge.

Bottom / Right -- Float bridge #3 as seen from the river end. All float bridges were retired in 1973.

Bottom / Left -- The Central Railroad of New Jersey maintained a blacksmith shop dedicated to the repair of the float bridges.

Top -- Float bridge repair shops at Jersey City. The building extending off the right side of the photograph is the yard office for transfer bridges. The freight house can barely be seen between the two buildings.

Middle / Top -- The yard office for transfer bridges.

Middle / Bottom -- Directly north of the ferry station was Dock #1. This photograph depicts Dock #1 as it would have appeared to a departing or arriving ferry. To the north of Dock #1 was Pier #2 and Pier #1. Both piers were built in 1878 and were constructed as open piers with tracks. Pier #1 was 71' x 494'. In 1914 a 36' x 65' one-story frame shelter for immigrants was constructed on Pier #1. Pier #1 had its tracks removed in 1933 and was retired in 1942. Pier #2 was 44' x 445'.

Bottom -- Constructed in 1909, Pier #5 extended 598' into the Hudson River. The pier was 66' wide. It was the first pier south of the station.

Top -- Pier #6 built in 1906 was 60' x 821'. There were two traveling gantry cranes on the pier. The cranes were retired in 1930. The Pier #5 shed can be seen in the lower left corner of the photograph.

Middle Three Photographs -- Pier #8 was built in 1883. The CNJ co-owned this coal pier with Burns Brothers, an anthracite wholesaler. This pier was known as the "Communipaw Pier." The photographs depict the elevated coal pier and the trestle leading to the pier.

Bottom -- Pier office for Pier #10. Pier #10 was constructed in 1907 and was 58' x 1,000'. The Central Railroad of New Jersey began filling in the marsh lands for the construction of piers 10-18 in 1906. The pier was rehabilitated in 1924. A bulk cement plant was constructed on this pier in 1934. The pier was retired in 1973.

Page 35 Middle / Right -- Crane at Pier #12. Pier #12 was an open 65' x 845' pier. The crane was retired in 1945 and the pier was retired in 1960.

Top -- In 1908 the CNJ built a 30' x 51' building near Pier #11 to serve as an employee restaurant. Pier #11 was constructed in 1912 and was 133' x 903'. A 125' x 883' covered shed was built on the pier for lighterage service. The pier was retired in 1973.

Middle / Left -- Pier #14, circa 1913-1915, was 133' x 755' with a 125' x 739' covered shed. Retired in 1973.

Bottom -- Dock #11 yards foreman's office.

store   asbestors   Paint

Page 36 -- Around 1912 the Central Railroad of New Jersey leased from the Boat Repair Corporation a large marine repair facility located just south of the CNJ piers and docks at Jersey City. In 1928 the CNJ purchased the property. Due to the fact that modern steel marine equipment required less maintenance than the old wooden equipment, the railroad sold the facilities to the Tug & Barge Supply Company in 1955 for $500,000.

The photographs depicted on this page captured two unidentified railroad ferry boats, a CNJ tug boat, and several marine repair facilities shop buildings.

Page 37 -- The Central Railroad of New Jersey ferry the *Lakewood* serves as a backdrop to a flag raising ceremony at the marine repair yard on September 16, 1940. Collection of James D. Brownback.

Top -- Jersey City Terminal Complex general yard master's office.

Middle / Left -- Passenger yard master's office.

Middle / Right -- Tower "B" was constructed in 1914. This 15' x 30' brick tower contained 47 levers and controlled the entrance to Communipaw Engine Terminal. The tower was retired in 1958 due to three main factors: the end of Baltimore and Ohio service, the revision of the CNJ passenger train service schedule, and the elimination of the south coach yard.

Bottom -- Tower "A" was constructed in 1915. This 19' x 71' brick tower contained 179 levers and controlled the throat of the Jersey Terminal Complex. Fifty-nine switch levers were abandoned in 1961. The tower closed on April 30, 1967.

Communipaw

The first station built at this location was on the eastbound side of the tracks in 1868. In 1891 a stone station was constructed on the westbound side. An island platform with a shelter was built between the main line tracks in 1910. The shelter was removed from the platform in 1958 and the overhead bridge was razed in the fall of 1983.

Top -- A view of Communipaw station depicting the stone westbound station of 1891 and the island platform of 1910. Circa 1950. Collection of William Krug.

Middle / Right -- Communipaw island platform and shelter. The access steps from the overhead bridge are visible.

Page 39 Middle / Left -- Office and quarters for engineers.

Page 39 Bottom -- Rest rooms for P&R (Philadelphia & Reading Railroad) trainman.

Top -- Coaling station at the Communipaw engine terminal.

Claremont

Claremont was established as a station stop in 1868. In 1892 an additional shelter was constructed. The station was closed in April of 1954 and was demolished.

Middle -- The original 1868 Claremont station area as it appeared around 1915.

Bottom -- Claremont station complex, circa 1950, showing the 1892 shelter and the remains of the ornate watchbox. Collection of William Krug.

Top -- Phillip Street tower was built in 1911-1912 as a 12' x 30' two-story brick building. The tower contained 47 levers and controlled the entrance to the Clermont freight yards and the Lehigh Valley Railroad's National Dock branch crossing.

Van Nostrand Place

Van Nostrand Place was established as a station stop in 1887. There is conflicting data on when the first station was constructed. The ICC states 1892, yet other sources have stated 1887 and 1891. The agency was discontinued in 1952. In 1958 the station was torn down at which time eastbound and westbound shelters were erected. These shelters were razed in 1972.

Middle / Top -- Van Nostrand Place Station.

Greenville

The Central Railroad of New Jersey, during the mid to late 1860s, built several stations that were nearly identical. This design became known as the "standard" CNJ station building. These standard stations were two-story frame 21' x 51' buildings. Greenville received a standard station in 1866.

On May 11, 1869 at 10:45 PM the station burned. The station was quickly rebuilt and served the CNJ for an additional 95 years until it was torn down in 1964.

Between 1964 and 1967 a simple shelter was used as the Greenville station. Greenville station stop was officially abolished on April 30, 1967.

Middle / Bottom -- The Greenville passenger station.

Bottom -- The overhead footbridge at Greenville was built in 1882 and was rebuilt in 1914. The bridge had a span of 87' 4" and was 5'8" wide.

Bayonne

East 49th Street, Bayonne

This location was established as a station stop in 1867 under the name of Pamrapo. A 21' x 51' two-story frame passenger station was built in 1878. The station was constructed using the standard CNJ station plan. Therefore the station would have looked similar to the Greenville station. Somewhere between 1889 and 1892 the station was renamed East 49th Street, Bayonne. With the construction of the East 45th Street, this station was abandoned on April 19, 1918.

East 45th Street, Bayonne

On April 19, 1918 the East 45th Street station replaced the East 49th Street station. The westbound station was a 20' x 50' one-story frame building. The agency closed in April, 1954. The station was demolished during the relocation and upgrade of the Center Street overhead bridge in 1961.

The 1918 eastbound shelter was replaced with the relocation of the sewer line in 1954. Both the eastbound and westbound side received new shelters in 1961.

On April 30, 1967 the station abandoned and both shelters were soon thereafter removed.

Top -- The westbound East 45th Street station. Collection of William Krug.

East 33rd Street, Bayonne

Originally known as Bayonne, this station stop was established in 1865-66. A standard CNJ station was built on the westbound side. The station was demolished and replaced with a shelter in 1962. The shelter was removed around 1979.

A station was built on the east-

bound side in 1901. This station was rebuilt into the main ticket agency in 1962 with the demolition of the westbound standard station. The station was razed in 1969. The East 33rd Street station was abandoned on August 6, 1978.

Page 42 Middle / Top -- The westbound standard CNJ station at East 33rd Street. Collection of William Krug.

East 22nd Street, Bayonne

Established in the mid to late 1860s as Centerville, the station was constructed on the eastbound side in 1878. The station was a 17' x 37' two-story frame building. The station was demolished in 1957 and was replaced with a shelter. The 1904 westbound station was converted into an open shelter. This shelter was razed in 1970 and replaced with a steel shed. East 22nd Street station was abandoned on August 6, 1978.

Page 42 Middle / Bottom -- The eastbound station at East 22nd Street. Collection of William Krug.

Page 42 Bottom / Left -- Railroad employee bunkhouses at East 22nd Street, Bayonne were known as "Car-ville."

Page 42 Bottom / Middle -- The railroad maintained engine facilities at East 22nd Street. The water town depicted in this photograph was built in 1900. The roundhouse can be seen behind the water tower.

Page 42 Bottom / Right -- The sand tower is adjacent to the East 22nd Street 17 stall roundhouse. The roundhouse was built in 1908 with an 80' turntable. It was abandoned in 1933. A coaling station was also built at this location in 1888 and was rebuilt during the construction of the round-house in 1908. A 136' x 25' two-story freight house was also constructed at this location. The freight house burned sometime in the 1960s. The East 22nd Street facilities served the Port Johnston coal docks and several industrial branches.

West 8th Street, Bayoone

Bergen Point was established as a station in 1864. Like Pamrapo, Bayonne, and Centerville, the CNJ changed the name some-time between the years 1889 and 1892 to West 8th Street. A standard station was built on the westbound side.

In 1891 a new westbound 94' x 37' stone station was constructed. This station was closed and remodeled shortly after World War II. It reopened for the traveling public on September 15, 1948.

A small 10' x 33' one-story frame station with a canopy was constructed on the east-bound side in 1903. In 1906 a pedestrian underpass was built to connect the two sta-tions. The eastbound station was demolished in 1971.

Top -- Section house at West 8th Street.

Middle -- The 1891 stone westbound sta-tion as seen from the eastbound platform.

Bottom -- The eastbound staton with its long canopy. The roof of the west-bound station is visable behind the east-bound station.

Top -- "BV" tower built at West 8th Street in 1903. The tower contained 15 levers and controlled freight leads to the East 22nd Street yard and the Port Johnston piers. This tower was replaced in 1926 with a 47 lever tower. In 1973 the tower was renamed "HOOK."

Middle / Top -- This 22' x 61' frame freight house replaced the original freight house at West 8th Street in 1903. The freight house was consolidated with the East 22nd Street freight house during the Great Depression of the 1930s.

Middle / Bottom -- The assistant yard masters office at Avenue Yard.

Avenue A, Bayonne

During the mid-1800s the area of Bayonne along the Newark Bay began to grow as a residential community. By 1885 the growth seemed sufficient for the CNJ to construct a one-story frame station on the westbound side of the tracks. However, by 1915, Avenue A was off the official CNJ station list. The station was razed in 1925 during the elevation of the tracks for the new Newark Bay Bridge.

The area south of the tracks began to industrialize after the turn of the twentieth century. The CNJ maintained a small yard at this location for that reason.

Bottom / Left -- This photograph may be the only known depiction of the Avenue A station.

Bottom / Right -- The yard master's office at Avenue Yard.

Port Johnston

Port Johnston served as the CNJ main tidewater coal terminal until Pier #18 was constructed at the Jersey City Terminal Complex in 1919. The first pier at Port Johnston was constructed in 1865 using fill from Bergen Point cut. Port Johnston served the CNJ until the early 1920s. The entire area was abandoned by 1939.

Top -- Port Johnston coal and dock office.

Top / Right -- Yard master's office at Port Johnston.

Middle -- Coal pier leased to the Johnston Coal Company.

Newark Bay Bridge

Since the first bridge was erected in 1864, the Newark Bay Bridge became a topic of great debate over whether or not it obstructed maritime traffic and industrial growth to the north of the bridge. Only three years after its opening, the New Jersey Assembly held an inquiry into the objections to the bridge. Although a tunnel was suggested several times, it was never constructed due to the enormous expense. In 1875 the cost of a tunnel was estimated at $6,000,000. By 1916 the price tag had ballooned to $100,000,000! The CNJ did replace the bridge several times; 1887, 1903, and 1924-1926, and with each replacement the draw span and height was increased. In the early 1980s a large portion of the bridge was destroyed, ending the obstruction controversies.

The first bridge was a low level trestle designed by CNJ chief engineer James Moore. The draw was 216 feet. The cost of the bridge

Bottom -- A view of the third 1903 bridge to cross the Newark Bay.

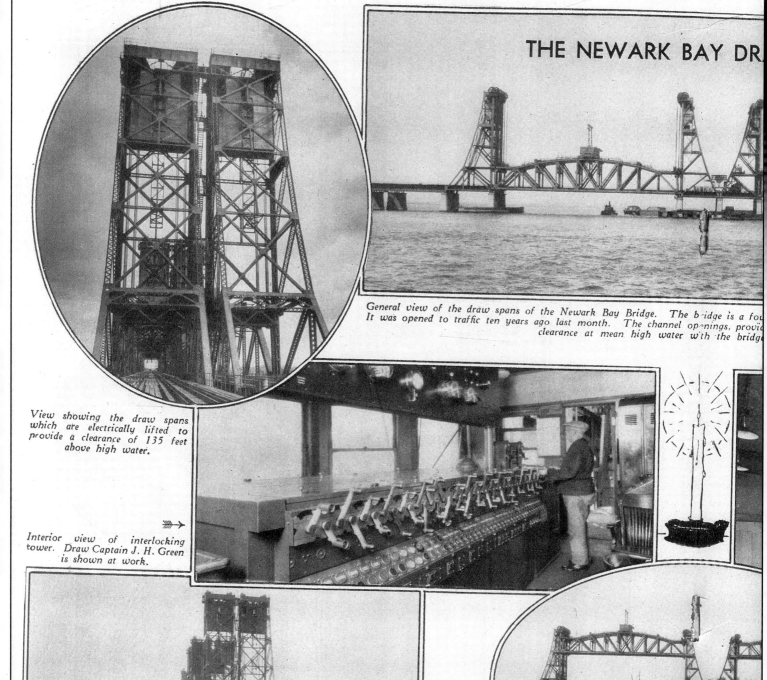

THE NEWARK BAY DR[...]

General view of the draw spans of the Newark Bay Bridge. The bridge is a fou[...]
It was opened to traffic ten years ago last month. The channel openings, provi[...]
clearance at mean high water with the bridg[...]

View showing the draw spans which are electrically lifted to provide a clearance of 135 feet above high water.

Interior view of interlocking tower. Draw Captain J. H. Green is shown at work.

View showing the old and new Newark Bay Bridge taken just prior to the opening of the new bridge in 1926.

The draw raised to allow ships to p[...]

was $319,500. This bridge was kept in the open position and lowered by hand cranks when needed. $12,000 per year was required for repairs and maintenance.

    The second bridge, built in 1887, had a 217' draw and was powered by steam. The third bridge contained two 85' Scherzer rolling lifting spans set back to back. In 1905 additional trackage was laid leading to the draw spans to allow for slow moving coal trains destined for Port Johnston. At the same time "BD" tower was built between the two spans. "BD" tower was a 12' x 14' frame building and contained 23 levers. The 1903 bridge remained in service until 11:00 AM, Friday April 24, 1926.

RK BAY DRAWBRIDGE.

ge. *The bridge is a four-track structure, 7411 feet long, costing $14,000,000.* *channel openings, provided by the draw, are 200 feet and 125 feet. The under-* *h water with the bridges closed is 35 feet.*

Rocking tower used to carry power cables from top of towers to movable spans.

Electrical switch control room for power operation of the bridge.

One of the motors which are used to operate the draw.

In 1923 work began on the fourth and final CNJ bridge to cross Newark Bay. The City of Newark challenged the CNJ's right to construct the bridge in court. The Supreme Court ruled in favor of the CNJ. The new bridge was a high-elevated with four vertical lifts. "DY" tower, constructed in the middle of the four lift spans, took over the control of the bridge and surrounding track. Although the bridge opened for service on April 24, 1926, the official opening ceremony did not take place until April 27th. Demolition of the bridge began in the early 1980s.

Page 46 & 47 -- Photographs from December, 1936, issue of the Reading - Jersey Central Magazine of the fourth 1926 Newark Bay bridge.

Top and Middle / Right -- Two views of the 1903 Newark Bay Bridge.

Singer's

To accommodate the employees of the Singer Sewing Machine Company which built a factory alongside the CNJ tracks just north of the Elizabethport Station, the CNJ created a station stop at the factory. In 1908 an overhead foot bridge was erected by the railroad. The foot bridge was built by Gueber Engineering Company and shipped to the site in pieces where the railroad forces assembled the bridge. Main line platforms were also installed. Singer's was eliminated as a station stop with the elevation of the tracks for the new 1926 Newark Bay Bridge.

Middle / Left -- The overhead foot bridge at Singer's.

Elizabethport Shops

Bottom -- Between 1902 and 1903 a 25 stall brick roundhouse with a 70 foot turntable was constructed. This is a view of that roundhouse in 1943. Just nine years later the roundhouse would be abandoned and demolished. Collection of James D. Brownback.

Elizabethport Shops

Top / Left -- The rear of the roundhouse.

Top / Right -- The locomotive coaling station was built in 1903 - 1904. It had a capacity of 800 tons. There was one sand chute and four coal chutes per side. It was demolished in 1953.

Middle / Left -- The 100,000 gallon water tank and water softner.

Middle / Right & Bottom / Left -- Two additional views of the coaling station.

Bottom / Right -- This water tower held salt water.

Top / Left -- The pattern storage house was a 42' x 82' concrete and brick building built in 1904.

Top / Right -- The lumber storage yard.

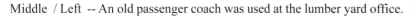

Middle / Left -- An old passenger coach was used at the lumber yard office.

Middle / Right / Top -- The cushion cleaning, dyeing and upholstering shop was built in 1903.

Middle / Right / Bottom -- In 1903 the 84' x 301' blacksmith house was built.

Bottom / Left -- Built during the 1903 Elizabethport shops improvement program, the power house was a 170' x 178' brick building.

Bottom / Right -- The arrow on the right points to the electric shop and storage building. The arrow on the left points to an old passenger car body being used as an office.

Top / Left and Top / Right -- The machine erecting and boiler shop was a brick 155' x 701' building erected in 1901. The building was used by New Jersey Transit into the 1990s. In June, 1997, the shop building was demolished.

Middle / Top / Left -- In 1912 the CNJ constructed a 179' x 600' brick building that served as the freight car repair shop. The shop had a capacity of 4,000 cars per month.

Middle / Top / Right -- The passenger car repair shop.

Middle / Bottom -- The transfer table was used by the locomotive and passenger car repair shops.

Bottom / Left -- The oil house was built in 1902.

Bottom / Right -- The freight transfer house was 28' x 58' and was built in 1906.

Top -- An aerial view of the Central Railroad of New Jersey facilities at Elizabethport, circa 1915. Just out of view is Singer's Bridge. Singers bridge would be right around the bend from the track that goes off the top of the photograph. The roundhouse, water tower, and water softner tower can be seen on the left side of the tracks in the middle of the photograph. On the right side of the tracks is the CNJ station. Interlocking towers "RU" and "RV" can be seen near the station. Following the track off the bottom of the photograph is the freight transfer office and a small portion of the freight transfer shed. This photograph illustrates why it became necessary to elevate this section of railroad. The CNJ passed through the residential neighborhood of Elizabethport with 12 grade crossings plus additional crossings for the Port Avenue branch and the Broadway branch.

Elizabethport Station

The first station at Elizabethport was built between 1865 and 1867. The station was located at Second Street which is closer to Singer's than the station which can be seen in the above photograph. The station was a standard CNJ station similar to the one built at Greenville. In 1873, with the construction of the Newark branch and the Perth Amboy branch, a wye was formed with the CNJ mainline several blocks below Singer's. A small shelter was built and designated as Amboy Junction. In 1877 the station at Second Street was moved to the wye.

In 1915 the Public Utility Commission began to hold hearings on eliminating the numerous grade crossings of the CNJ through Elizabethport. Fifteen years later the State of New Jersey passed the Davis Act, which divided the cost of the $9,000,000 project between the State and the CNJ into a 50-50 basis. Detailed plans were made and work finally began in 1931. Work was soon halted as the country felt the effects of the Great Depression. Work resumed on a scaled-back plan on November 14, 1936. The new plan was accomplished with a $5,400,000 Public Works Administration (PWA) grant.

During the grade crossing elimination plan, the wooden CNJ standard station was replaced with a modern brick station that was conservative in size and design, allowing it to fit into the lower budget of the new plan. This station was demolished in 1984-85. The project consolidated towers "RU" and "RV" into one tower known as "RU." In 1972 the tower was renamed "Port." Work was completed on the entire grade crossing elimination and new station facilities project on November 30, 1938.

ELIZABETHPORT GRADE CROSSING ELIMINATION NEARS COMPLETION

(At left) General view showing progress of construction of passenger station.

(Right) Eastbound platform and station under construction.

(Left) Laying tracks on new elevated roadbed east of the Newark Branch crossing.

View showing street underpass which replaces grade crossing.

ELIZABETHPORT, NEW JERSEY

Latest views of the improved facilities made possible by the combined efforts
of the C. R. R. of N. J., State of New Jersey and the Federal Government.

Top -- Views of the Elizabethport station from the November, 1939, issue of the Reading - Jersey Central Magazine.
Page 53 -- Construction photographs of from the new Elizabethport station and grade crossing elimination project. Photographs from the December, 1938, issue of the Reading - Jersey Central Magazine.

Spring Street, Elizabeth

The westbound station was constructed in 1869. This station was replaced with a 12' x 25' shelter in 1903. The eastbound station was built in 1891-92 and was used until it was demolished in 1951. A section of the canopy was retained until it burned in the mid 1970s.

Top / Left -- The eastbound Spring Street, Elizabeth station.

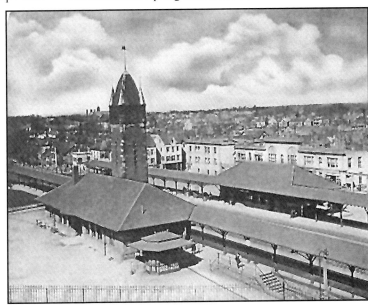

Middle -- The CNJ freight station at Elizabeth. The freight station, a 30' x 100' red brick building, was constructed using a Reading Railroad standard design in 1893. The freight station was closed in 1951.

Elizabeth

From 1839-1854, Jacob Seiple's hotel at Morris Avenue and Broad Street served as the Elizabeth station. A dedicated railroad station was constructed in 1854. The station was rebuilt in 1868.

In July, 1892, work began on elevating the CNJ tracks through Elizabeth. Two new elevated brick and stone Romanesque style stations were built at the time of track elevation. The westbound station was 25' x 65' and the eastbound station was 30' x 90' with an 87' clock tower.

On November 4, 1972 a derailed freight train demolished the westbound station. The eastbound station was closed on August 6, 1978 and is still standing.

Top / Right -- The elevated Elizabeth station. Both stations can bee seen in this aerial view. The building next to the eastbound station is a news stand. Collection of Benjamin L. Bernhart.

Bottom / Left and Right -- By 1915, the 1848 roundhouse was being used as a storeroom.

55

El Mora

Originaly established as West Elizabeth station in April of 1870. In the early 1880s the station was moved across the avenue so that it would no longer sit in the city of Elizabeth. Lower taxes was the motivation behind the move.

The westbound station, a frame two-story 17' x 55' building, was built in 1883. The station was razed in March, 1944, and replaced with a shelter. The 9' x 50' eastbound station was built in 1912. This station was replaced with a metal shelter in 1968.

Top / Left -- The westbound El Mora station.

Top / Right -- The easbound El Mora station.

Lorrain

In the mid-1890s the CNJ eastablished Lorrain as a station. In 1908 an eastbound non-agency station was constructed. The station was a 12' x 16' frame building with a canopy. It was demolished in 1968.

Middle -- Lorrain station, circa 1940. Collection of William Krug.

Roselle - Roselle Park

Bottom / Right -- The 1866-68 Roselle station at 42nd and Westfield Avenue. After it was closed in 1902 the CNJ rented the building as a dwelling.

Bottom / Left -- "QR" tower was built at Lorrain in 1910. It was a white brick 17' x 30' two-story building with 29 levers. The functions of Roselle tower were moved to "QR" tower in 1912. The tower was abandoned in 1949.

Top / Left -- The mission style 1902 eastbound Roselle station.

Top / Right -- The boiler house at Roselle was constructed by the CNJ in 1868.

The first station at this location was built at Hope Avenue and was known as Mulford. A standard CNJ station was constructed at 42nd & Westfield Avenue in 1867 and the name was changed to Roselle. New westbound and eastbound stations were built in 1902. Roselle was abandoned in 1978.

Aldene

The Lehigh Valley Railroad (LV) junctioned with the CNJ at Aldene. The first station was constructed in 1892 just east of the LV overpass. In 1913-14 new eastbound and westbound stations were constructed just west of the LV overpass. The westbound was a 24' x 44' frame station which became the Aldene yard office in 1954. The station was demolished in April, 1972. The eastbound station was a 16' x 30' one-story frame station. The station was sold in 1955 and the canopies were removed. In 1964 the eastbound station was demolished.

Middle -- The Aldene station, circa 1960. Collection of William Krug.

Cranford Junction

Cranford Junction was established as a junction with the Baltimore & Ohio Railroad in 1890. Between 1911 and 1914 the CNJ constructed a suburban coach yard and engine facilities at this location. The engine facilities were abandoned in April, 1954.

Bottom / Left -- The coaling tower was constructed in 1914.

Bottom / Right -- The track leading to the Cranford Junction turntable was built between the coaling tower and the water tower. In 1912 construction began on an 80' turntable and an 8-stall brick roundhouse. An ash pit was also built at Cranford Junction.

Page 58 -- Views of Cranford Junction from the August, 1941 issue of the Reading - Jersey Magazine

CRANFORD AND RARITAN

(Top left) Turntable and coal dock at Cranford. (Circle) Locomotive No. 108 taking water at Cranford. (Centre) The Raritan section gang. (Bottom, left to right) Fred Conover, section foreman, Section 17, Raritan; view along the right of way at Cranford showing XC tower; and L. R. Jones, gateman, Anderson Street, Raritan.

Top / Left -- "XC" tower at Cranford Junction was constructed around 1890. The tower was a wood frame building containing 26 levers. In 1891 this was increased to 32 levers. On September 29, 1907, a new 41 lever machine was installed. A new 10' x 22' white brick tower was built in 1912. The 1907 machine was moved from the old wood frame tower to the new brick tower. In 1973 the tower was renamed "EXCEE." This photograph depicts the 1912 tower.

Top / Right -- Two old CNJ passenger car bodies serve as offices at Cranford Junction.

Cranford

In 1839 a platform was erected in an open field and the station stop of "French House" was created. The first agency station was constructed in 1844. A standard CNJ station was built in 1865, at which time the 1844 station became the freight house. It was also around this time that the name of the station was changed to Cranford. On April 28, 1906, new eastbound and westbound stations were opened. The eastbound was a 21' x 71' one story brick and stone station with a tile roof. The westbound was a 15' x 22' building connected to the eastbound by a pedestrian underpass. During the 1927-30 track elevation project, Cranford received its fourth station. The station opened on August 11, 1929.

Middle -- A summer of 1942 view of the 1929 high-level station at Cranford. The ticket office and waiting room were located at ground level on the south side of the tracks. Collection of James D. Brownback.

Bottom / Left -- Freight crane near the Garwood freight station at Chestnut and North Avenue. The freight house was built in 1901 and retired in 1951. It was demolished during the 1961-62 grade crossing elimination program.

Garwood

Numerous small industries were located in Garwood. Garwood station was constructed in 1892 to serve the employees of the of these industries. The station was located on the eastbound track. The station was demolished in 1976 when it was replaced by a bus-type shelter.

Bottom / Right -- The Garwood station. Collection of William Krug.

Westfield

The first station at Westfield was established in 1839. It was manned by an Irishman who also sold candy and cakes. The station was destroyed by a devastating fire. A standard CNJ station was then constructed at Clark and Broad Streets. Peabody & Stearns constructed a new 26' x 74' westbound station in 1891. In 1912-13 a new 30' x 70' eastbound station was built. Both stations were sold to the town of Westfield

Top -- The 1869 standard CNJ station at Westfield. Collection of James D. Brownback.

Middle / Left / Top -- The 1891 westbound station at Westfield, circa 1939. Collection of James D. Brownback.

Middle / Right -- The 1912-13 eastbound station, circa 1939. Collection of James D. Brownback

in 1955. The stations were refurbished in 1986.

The Westfield freight house was located on the south side of the tracks. The 23' x 90' one-story frame freight house was built in 1892. It was retired in 1951 and demolished in 1968.

Middle / Left / Bottom -- A 1937 view of the tracks at Westfield looking west towards Fanwood. The westbound 1891 station can be seen on the right side of the photograph. The freight house is on the left side. Collection of James D. Brownback.

Bottom -- Bridge 19[85] near Westfield.

Fanwood

The original route of the CNJ by-passed Fanwood by going through Scotch Plains. However, the route through Scotch Plains had an undesirable grade. To reduce the grade the CNJ began constructing a new line in 1865.

In January, 1868, a standard CNJ station with additional large gables was opened at Fanwood. Fanwood was named after Frances (Fanny) Colles, the wife of CNJ president John Taylor Johnston. The 1868 westbound station was sold to the town of Fanwood in 1965.

In 1897 a 18' x 30' one-story frame station was built on the westbound side. This station was razed in 1986.

Top -- Fanwood received a more elaborate and ornate version of the standard CNJ station.

Netherwood, Plainfield

Eastablished as a station in 1874, Netherwood was a suburb of Plainfield. The original 1874 station was replaced in 1892-93 with a 20' x 57' station on the eastbound side. The westbound station was built in 1913.

Just north of the Netherwood station was the country home of the CNJ's president, John Taylor Johnston.

Middle -- The Netherwood station.

Plainfield

Established as a station stop in 1839, Plainfield received its first station in 1839-40. The station was damaged and fell apart in 1849. In the summer of 1851 the station was rebuilt and relocated. This station remained until the track relocation project of 1873.

A new westbound station opened on May 17, 1875. This station was a two-story brick 140' x 41' with two one-story 50' x 23' wings. The cost of the station was $30,000. The station was remodeled in 1952. During the remodeling, the second story was removed. In 1981 the station was leased to the city of Plainfield and used as an art center.

Ground was broken on July 31, 1900, for an eastbound station that was completed in early 1901. The eastbound station was a 26' x 91' two-story brick station connected to the westbound station by a pedestrian underpass. The eastbound passenger station was built on the grounds of the original freight station which was closed when a new freight station was built in 1895. The new freight station was a 45' x 157' one-story brick building.

Bottom -- "JA" was constructed at Plainfield in 1905. The tower was a 12' x 22' two-story brick building with 29 levers. The tower was closed in 1953.

CENTRAL R. R. STATION, PLAINFIELD, N. J.   68997

Top -- Two views of the 1874-75 west-bound Plainfield station.

Middle / Top -- The eastbound 1900-01 Plainfield station.

Grant Avenue, Plainfield

By the request of local residents, Grant Avenue became a station stop on September 28, 1885. The station was built on land donated to the railroad. Residents also donated $3,000 to the project. The station was sold in 1957.

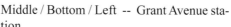

Middle / Bottom / Left -- Grant Avenue station.

Dunellen

Middle / Bottom / Right -- Three water tanks were constructed at Dunellen in 1875-79. New watering facilities were built in 1921.

Bottom -- The standard CNJ 1868 station at Dunellen.

Clinton Avenue, Plainfield

CNJ president, John Taylor Johnston estbalished this location as a station stop in 1872 with the name "Evona." Eva was the youngest daughter of Mr. Johnston. The name was changed to Clinton Avenue in January, 1895. A station simular to the embellished CNJ standard station of Fanwood was constructed in 1872. The station was demolished in 1957.

Dunellen

Established in 1840 as New Market. Charles Pope's store at Gove Street was used as the waiting room until 1868. Shortly after the Civil War ended, the CNJ began buying land in the area under their development company, the Central New Jersey Land Improvement Company. In May of 1868 a town was laid out.

CNJ president Mr. Johnston named the community in honor of Ellen Betts, a wife of a New York friend. In Scotch "Dun" means hill, so the town was Ellen's Hill.

In August, 1868, a standard CNJ station was constructed on the westbound side. The station and ground were sold in 1953 to a developer. The station was demolished and a shopping center was built. The location of the station did not fit into the track elevation project that began in 1953 and was finished in 1956.

The eastbound station was a 16' x 31' one-story frame station that was built in 1898. This station was also removed during the elevation project of 1953. On December 10, 1955 the new elevated Dunellen station opened. The 1899 freight house, the 1904 "DX" (aka "DN") tower, and the 1875-79 engine facilities were all abandoned and removed during the elevation project.

Green Brook

Green Brook was not a station stop, but was a very important watering facility that was established in 1859. Track pans were installed between 1888 and 1893. After a devestating fire, the facilities were rebuilt in November of 1929 at a cost of $54,000. The facility was abandoned in the 1950s.

Top -- The stone bridge over the Green Book was built in 1852. It received two additional arches in 1904.

Middle / Left --The pump and boiler house was built in 1910 at Green Brook.

Middlesex

Established around 1893 with the name of Lincoln. A statue of president Lincoln stood on the station grounds. The name was later changed to Middlesex. In 1893 a 16' x 20' one-story frame station was built. The station received an addition and a new roof design sometime after 1915. The station was demolished in 1972.

Middle / Right -- The original appearance of the Lincoln station.

Bottom -- The rebuilt appearance.

Bound Brook

Eastablished as Yellow Tavern in 1840, the station was located on the east side of the brook. Around 1842 a new station was established and the name was changed to Bound Brook. Another new station was constructed in 1859-60. An embellished form of the CNJ standard station was built at a new location in 1872.

As in many of the surrounding communities, the CNJ crossed many of streets at grade. Plans began in 1902 to eliminate many of the grade crossings through Bound Brook. Work did not begin on this project until 1911. A new modern Bound Brook station was included in this plan.

On August 10, 1913, new eastbound and westbound stations were opened. The stations were of a Reading Railroad design.

Top -- The embellished standard CNJ station at Bound Brook. Collection of William Krug.

Middle -- The 1913 Reading Railroad design eastbound station.

Calco

In 1915 the Calco Chemical Company plant was built and the CNJ established a station stop for the plant employees. In 1941 the tracks were elevated and new shelters were built.

Bound Brook Junction

The Reading Railroad's New York line met the CNJ at Bound Brook Junction. Several of the stations along the New York line were designed using the CNJ standard station plan as a foundation. These station include Pennington, Skillman, Belle Mead and Weston.

Manville - Finderne

First established as at station stop at Dun's Landing in 1851. Due to very slow ticket sales the CNJ abandoned this stop in 1854. The station was restablished in 1868 under the name Finderne. A 17' x 33' two-story frame station was constructed on the westbound side. In 1968 the station was sold to Central Avenue Corporation. The station was demolished in 1972 in order to extend industrial sidings. A shelter was built on the eastbound side in 1916.

Bottom / Left -- Bridge 32[87] at Finderne Avenue just east of the station. The bridge was built by the Phoenix Bridge Company in 1914. Note the horse walking across the bridge.

Bottom / Right -- Manville - Finderne station. Manville was added to the name of the station in 1913. Collection of William Krug.

Somerville

Somerville was established as a station stop in 1842. The first passenger train travelled through Somerville on January 2, 1842. The train consisted of an engine and two coaches, one of which was named "Essex." Three regular trains were then scheduled between Somerville and Jersey City. When it was time for a train to arrive or depart Somerville, the station agent, Bernard Stearns, would ring an iron bell atop a tall pole in front of the station.

Top -- The Manville branch was built in 1913-14, requiring this long 312.5 foot bridge over the Raritan River. It was built by the Pennsylvania Steel Co. and erected by Richards & Gaston.

Replacing the first station, a two-story frame station opened on November 28, 1856. The station was located between the westbound and eastbound tracks. There was a water tank at both ends of the station. On May 10, 1867, a fire broke out in the frame to the water tank on the west side of the station. The fire quickly spread to the station, destorying everything on the station grounds.

A temporary one-story frame station was then built. This station served Somerville for 23 years until a new station was built in 1890. The fourth station was a 30' x 36' two-story stone and frame station. The sandstone came from the quarries at Stockton, New Jersey. The total cost of the station was $15,000. It was officialy opened on November 20, 1890 with a grand celebration. Somerville's local newspaper, the Somerset Messenger - Gazette, described the 1890 celebration as follows:

The old National Guard outfit, Company H, marched down to Depot square and fired 13 volleys to start the program. All locomotives that could be assembled around the railyards had their whistles tied down and screeched out 140 pounds of steam. Three hundred railroad torpedoes were placed on the tracks and train shuttled around banging off these dynamite caps. A huge bonfire was lighted. Old timbers and tar roofing torn from the old (station) building provided the fuel. The fire alarm was kept blowing at intervals. Company H had meanwhile deployed and started skirmish fighting in the streets around the station, using blank ammunition. A couple of thousand folks who could stand excitement milled around and shouted.

In 1924 the station grounds were modernized and pedestrian tunnels and platforms were built. The tracks were regraded, yet the station building itself remained nearly the same. In 1985 New Jersey Transit sold the station and it was converted into a resaurant.

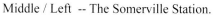

Middle / Left -- The Somerville Station.

Middle / Right / Top -- The 1887 Centre Street Bridge #34[48]. It was located just east of the station.

Middle / Right / Bottom -- Somerville's track scale.

Bottom -- Coaling platform and old car body.

Page 66 -- Views around Somerville from the June, 1941, issue of the Reading - Jersey Magazine.

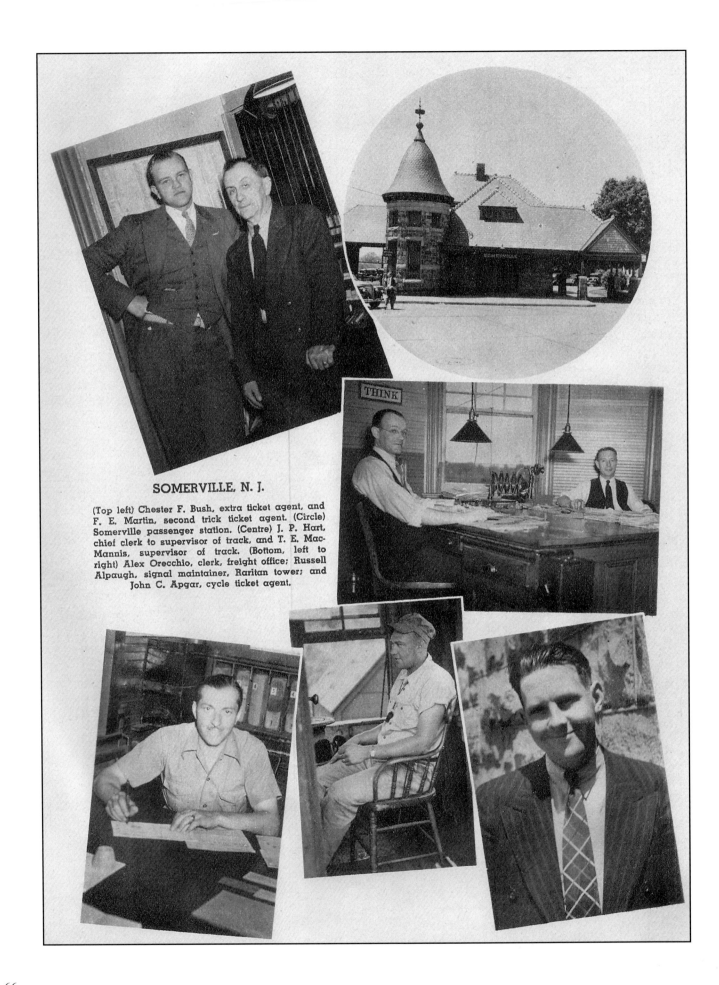

SOMERVILLE, N. J.

(Top left) Chester F. Bush, extra ticket agent, and F. E. Martin, second trick ticket agent. (Circle) Somerville passenger station. (Centre) J. P. Hart, chief clerk to supervisor of track, and T. E. Mac-Mannis, supervisor of track. (Bottom, left to right) Alex Orecchio, clerk, freight office; Russell Alpaugh, signal maintainer, Raritan tower; and John C. Apgar, cycle ticket agent.

RARITAN FACES

(Above) Turntable at Raritan. (Upper right) Joe Stonik, day assistant foreman, round house. (Right) Raritan station. (Below) E. T. Lightcop, towerman. (Circle) Wall G. Hanson, gateman at Anderson Street.

Raritan

Raritan was originally established as Somerville Water Power. A station was built shortly after 1851. A 25' x 68' one-story stone station was constructed on the eastbound side in 1892. The 1892 station building was moved several feet to the south in 1924-26 to allow for the addition of two tracks. In 1986 the station was leased by New Jersey Transit to the borough of Raritan to be used as their offices.

Page 67 --Views around Raritan from the July 1941 Reading - Jersey Central Magazine. The engine terminal, turntable and coach yard was built in 1923-25 to replace the facilities at Somerville.

Top -- The Raritan station.

North Branch

Although established as a station stop in 1848 the first station was not constructed until 1850. A second station was built in 1860 and a third station was built in 1892.-93. The third station sat on the eastbound side and was a 19' x 25' two-story stone and frame building. On January 8, 1970, the station was destroyed by fire. A bus-type shelter was then built.

Middle / Top -- Bridge #39^{07} over the North Branch of the Raritan River was built in 1876 by Jas. Smith. The first bridge at this location was built in 1850.

Middle / Bottom -- North Branch station.

White House

White House was established as a station stop in the late 1840s. The first station was built in 1850. In 1892-93 a 27' x 73' one-story stone station was constructed. In 1981 the station was sold and converted into the local public library.

Bottom -- Rear view of the White House station. The water tower next to the station was built in 1901 and had the capacity of 48,000 gallons of water.

Lebanon

Established around 1852, Lebanon received its first train station in 1855-56. A new 20' x 59' one-story frame station was constructed on the eastbound side in 1900.

Top / Left -- Lebanon station was sold to the High Iron Company for use as offices.

Annandale

With the construction of a station in 1852, Clinton station stop was established. The name was changed to Annandale in 1870-71. A 26' x 47' one-story frame station was built in 1900. This station was replaced in November of 1935 with a station that had cost only $227.

Top / Right -- A rear view of the station that was built at Annandale in 1900.

Middle / Left / Top -- The 25' x 81' Annandale freight house was built in 1883 replacing the 1871 freight house.

Middle / Left / Bottom -- One of the main commodities shipped from Annandale was peaches. The CNJ even maintained a peach shelter at this location.

High Bridge

In 1856 a station was built near the Union Iron Works. The station received its name from the bridge that crossed over the South Branch of the Raritan River just east of town. The bridge was 105' high and 1300' long. The majority of this bridge was filled in with dirt during the early 1860s.

On July 24, 1869 at 3:40 PM the High Bridge station was set

ablaze by a spark from steam locomotive #69. A new station was built that same year. The 1869 station was converted into offices and a section house with the construction of a 21' x 66' one-story frame with stucco station in 1910-11.

Middle / Right -- The High Bridge station, circa 1941. The roof of the 1869 station can just barely be seen in the upper left corner.

Bottom -- The station and freight house, circa 1940. Collection of James D. Brownback.

Glen Gardner

Established as a station stop known as Clarkville in 1852. It was re-named Spruce Run in November of 1864 and renamed again to Glen Gardner in the early 1870s to honor the Gardner Bros. chair factory. A standard CNJ station was constructed in 1868-69. The station was de-molished in 1956 and replaced with a shelter.

Top / Left -- The standard CNJ station at Glen Gardner, circa 1941. Collection of James D. Brownback.

Top / Right -- Glen Gardner station.

Middle -- The freight house at Glen Gardner was a 21' x 41' one-story frame building.

Hampton

New Hampton was established as a sta-tion stop in 1852. In 1856 the name was changed to Junction and by 1902 the name was changed to Hampton Junction. Around 1950 the junction was dropped from the name and the station was then known as Hampton. Hampton was the junction of the CNJ and the Delaware, Lackawanna and Western (DL&W) Rail-road.

The station was built in the 1850s us-ing a basic DL&W design. The station was jointly owned by the two railroads. Hampton became a very important inter-change, handling 700 to 800 cars per day during the 1870s. For this reason the CNJ maintained a large rail yard and engine facilities at this location.

Bottom -- The co-owned CNJ and DL&W station at Hampton.

Top / Left -- Hampton Station, circa 1941. Collection of James D. Brownback.

Top / Right -- Bunk shanty on coal trestle in Hampton yards.

Middle / Left -- Yard masters office in Hampton yards.

Middle / Right -- Turntable and old box car bodies used by car inspectors at Hampton.

Ludlow - Asbury

Established as Asbury in 1852-54. Ludlow was added to the name by 1915. In 1900 a new 20' x 52' one-story stone station was built.

Bottom -- Ludlow - Asbury station, circa 1941. Collection of James D. Brownback.

Page 72 / Top / Left -- Ludlow - Asbury Station.

Valley

Eastablished as Bethlehem station stop in 1852. The name was change to Valley around 1855. The original station was destroyed by fire on Febuary 8, 1870 from sparks emitted from a passing steam locomotive. A new station was built in 1871. In 1893 a 12' x 16' frame shelter was built. Valley was abandoned as a station stop in 1933.

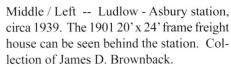
Middle / Left -- Ludlow - Asbury station, circa 1939. The 1901 20' x 24' frame freight house can be seen behind the station. Collection of James D. Brownback.

Bloomsbury

Seventeen years after Bloomsbury was established as a station stop a standard CNJ station was constructed in 1869. The station was sold in the early 1960s and was demolished in 1968.

Middle / Right -- Bloomsbury Station.

Bottom / Right -- The 1901 Bloomsbury pumping station pumped water from the Musconetcong River.

Springtown

Established as a station stop in 1852. A two-story brick station was built in the 1870-80s. The agency was closed by 1900 and the station was abandoned around 1932.

Bottom / Left -- Springtown station.

Vulcanite

To serve the local cement company, the CNJ established as station stop at Vulcanite in 1894. A 19' x 84' one-story concrete passenger and freight station was constructed in 1915. The cement company closed after World War II at which time the CNJ retired the Vulcanite station. The station was demolished in 1966.

Top -- Bridge 67[97] just east of the Vulcanite station.

Middle / Left / Top -- Vulcanite Station.

Greens Bridge

Greens Bridge was not a station stop for the CNJ, but an important and impressive bridge over the Lopatcong Creek and the Morris Canal. The original 1852 bridge was replace in 1865 with a 5-span stone arch bridge. Each span was 75'6". Sidney Billon constructed the bridge. The total cost of the bridge was $100,000.

Middle / Right and Middle / Left / Bottom -- Two views of Bridge 70[44] over the Lopatcong Creek and Morris Canal at Greens Bridge.

Black Dan's Cut, Phillipsburg

The worlds first electrically operated semaphore signal was placed in operation at Black Dan's Cut, near Phillipsburg in 1893. The signal was invented by J. W. Lattig of Bethlehem, Pennsylvania. Mr. Lattig was associated with the National Switch and Signal Company of Easton, PA.

The signal worked by means of a stout phosphor bronze wire operating over a drum forming part of the motor assembly, the spectacle casting was moved by a balance lever and up and down rod to "proceed" position. The arm returned to "stop" by gravity.

Bottom -- The electric semaphore at Black Dan's cut. Collection of James D. Brownback.

Top / Left -- The first coaling facility at Phillipsburg was built in 1865. This coaling station was replaced in 1885 and then again in 1909. The 1909 coaling tower had an extension over the mainline tracks. The coaling tower was abandoned in 1948 and removed in 1952.

Top / Right -- The building behind the water tank is the machine shop.

Middle / Left -- Carpenter Shop.

Middle / Right -- The yard masters office was a 17' x 32' two-story frame building built in 1888. It was replaced in 1945.

Bottom / Left -- The Market Street shanty.

Bottom / Right -- The west elevation of the coaling tower.

Top -- In 1852 an octagonal shape stone engine house with the capacity of 16 steam locomotives was built. This engine house was replaced in 1865-66 with a 15-stall roundhouse. Needing additional engine facilities the CNJ built a second 15-stall roundhouse in 1869. Both of these roundhouses were demolished in 1909 when a new 10-stall roundhouse was constructed with a 65' turntable. The roundhouse was abandoned in 1937 and demolished in 1938. The functions of the Phillipsburg roundhouse were assumed by the Bethlehem, Pennsylvania, engine terminal.

Middle / Top -- Located next to the 1909 roundhouse was the shop foreman's office. An old passenger car body can also be seen in the photograph. Most likely the car body was being used as an office.

Middle / Bottom -- The 62' x 103' one-story brick machine shop was built in 1866. In August, 1936, the CNJ was granted approval for abandonment of the machine shop. The CNJ officially abandoned the machine shop in 1937.

Bottom -- The first freight station at Phillipsburg was constructed in 1852. This building was moved to Main Street and became a passenger car house in 1869. The CNJ then built two freight houses, one on each side of the tracks, just east of Main Street. The two freight houses were replaced with a 35' x 151' one-story frame station in 1878. This photograph depicts the 1878 freight house.

Phillipsburg Station

The first station at Phillipsburg was built in 1852. The original station burned in 1857. An enlarged CNJ standard station opened in 1859 on the south side of the tracks between Market Street and the Delaware River bridge. In 1874 an additional baggage room was constructed onto the station. The CNJ moved into the DL&W station in the late 1890s, at which time the 1859 station was demolished.

The DL&W station was built around 1868 on the west side of Market Street. The station was located at the junction of the DL&W and the CNJ. In 1914-15 the DL&W and the CNJ constructed a jointly owner station.

The new station was a 57' x 61' two-story brick building located at Main Street. The last DL&W passenger train to leave the station was on July 15, 1941. The CNJ stopped using the station in 1959. It was sold in June, 1960, to Phillipsburg Pharmacy, Inc. The station still stands today.

Leading from the DL&W and CNJ station was a wooden walkway and stairs leading to the Belvidere & Delaware Railroad station. The station was located below the CNJ's bridge across the Delaware River. The B&D station was called Lehigh Junction.

The CNJ continued passenger service to Phillipsburg until April 30, 1967. When passenger service was restored on May 20, 1974, a gravel platform was used as the station. Passenger service was once again discontinued on December 31, 1983.

Top -- The east elevation of the Phillipsburg station.

Middle / Top -- The west elevation.

Middle / Bottom -- The CNJ and the Reading Railroad, in cooperation, ran a through train from Harrisburg to New York. This train was known as the Queen of the Valley. In this 1942 photograph the Queen of the Valley has just arrived at Phillipsburg. The train is heading east from Harrisburg. Collection of James D. Brownback.

Bottom / Left -- Phillipsburg station, circa 1939. Collection of James D. Brownback.

Bottom / Right -- CNJ westbound train #193 arriving at Phillipsburg, circa 1939. Train #193, originated out of Newark, New Jersey. On Sundays the train would leave at 9:05 AM. The train then traveled to Jersey City. Leaving Jersey City it made station stops at Elizabethport, Elizabeth, Plainfield, Bound Brook, Somerville, and arrived at Phillipsburg at 10:48 AM. The train then proceeded to Bethlehem and on to Allentown where it terminated. Collection of James D. Brownback.

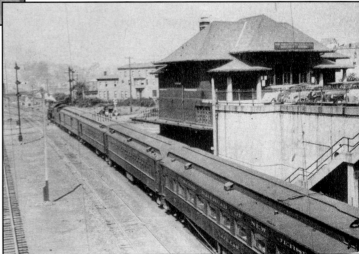

CHAPTER 5

EASTON TO SCRANTON, PA

Easton

The first Easton station opened on June 14, 1868. In 1885 the station was destroyed by fire. For the next four years, a passenger coach served as the station. In 1889 a unique one-story brick station was constructed. The station was built partly on the west end of the Lehigh River bridge. This station was a victim of arson on Labor Day, 1975. In October 1975 the station was razed.

Top -- The 1889 Easton station looking east towards New Jersey.

Middle / Right -- Easton station looking westward, circa 1939. Collection of James Brownback.

Page 78 / Top / Left -- The CNJ grain elevator at Easton.

Page 78 / Top / Right -- CNJ warehouse in Easton leased to Drake & Co.

Odenwelder

The CNJ did not maintain an agency or station at Odenwelder. Engine facilities were constructed at Odenwelder in the late 1860s and early 1870s.

Middle / Left -- The Easton freight station was built in 1889-90. It was originally built as a 30' x 131' one-story brick station. In 1913-14 a two-story addition was added.

Bottom -- The Easton freight station as seen from street level.

Glendon

It is unclear if Glendon ever had an active agency. The station was built pre-1885 and also served as a watchman shanty.

Island Park

Island Park shelter was constructed to serve the patrons of Island Park amusement park. Also nearby is Chain Dam Island.

Middle -- Watchman shanty and station at Glendon.

Bottom -- Island Park passenger shelter.

Freemansburg

Established as a station when a combined passenger and freight station was built in 1868. The station was a 19' x 65' one-story frame building. It was demolished in 1966.

Top -- The Freemansburg combination station.

Bethlehem

In 1868 Bethlehem was established as a station stop. Six years later, in April 1874, a large two-story brick station opened. Passenger service was discontinued from the station on August 18, 1967.

The Bethlehem Jaycees restored the sation in 1966-67. The station is still standing and is home to a restaurant.

Middle / Top -- Bethlehem station.

Bethlehem Junction

In 1867 a junction was formed with the CNJ and the South Bethlehem Branch of the Lehigh & New England (L&NE) Railroad. A one-story frame station was built in 1873. The CNJ discontinued Bethlehem Junction as a station stop on April 27, 1930.

Middle / Bottom -- Bethlehem Junction station.

Bottom / Left -- The three stall engine house and 65' turntable were built in 1871-72. The roundhouse was demolished in 1928.

Bottom / Right -- The 50,000 gallon water tower was built around 1888.

Top / Left -- Bridge #1 built in 1895.

Top / Right -- Bridge #3 over Lehigh River to Jeter Island.

Middle / Left / Top -- Bridge over Lehigh Canal built in 1889.

Middle / Right / Top -- Bridge #4 & #5. Bridge #5 was updated in 1917.

Middle / Left / Bottom -- Bridge #8 1/2 at Front Street.

Middle / Right / Bottom -- Bridge #10 built in 1889.

Bottom -- Ainyville branch bridge #2 built in 1895.

Allentown became a station stop in 1890. The one-story brick station with clock tower was opened on March 17, 1890. The station was also used by the Reading Railroad's Reading to Allentown trains. The last Reading Railroad train to use the station was on June 30, 1963. The last CNJ passenger train was on August 18, 1967. The station was used for a brief time by South Eastern Pennsylvania Transit Authority (SEPTA) during the 1970s.

At the peak of passenger service, 1,500 passengers per day were handled at Allentown. The Allentown station still stands today waiting for the revivial of train service.

Top / Left -- "Y" tower was built in 1890. The frame two-story tower was 12' x 20'. In 1895 it was rebuilt and a 32 lever mechanical interlocking machine installed. In 1902 it was rebuilt again. The tower was replace by "J" tower in 1926.

Top / Right -- Pump house near Allentown.

Middle / Right -- Crossing tower at Hamilton Street.

Middle / Left -- Philadelphia & Reading Railroad passenger coach #1080 awaits departure from the Allentown CNJ station at Hamilton Street. The photograph was taken at 3:30 PM, circa 1916.

Bottom -- Postcards of local railroad stations were common during the early 1900s. This postcard captured the splendor of the Allentown station.

Top / Left -- The Allentown freight station was built in 1890. This view of the freight station was taken around 1940. Collection of James D. Brownback.

Top / Right -- CNJ section house at Allentown.

Middle -- Stationery freight crane.

Gordon Street, Allentown
Established a station in 1890, a combination station was built in 1893. During the depression it was converted into a crew quarters for dinning car employees.

Front Street, Allentown
Front Street was established as a station stop in 1890. Although found on early timetables, Front Street station is not list by the ICC during the evaluation in 1915.

Bottom -- The 1868 Catasauqua station.

East Allentown
Before the Allentown Terminal Railroad was constructed in 1890 allowing trains to arrive into Allentown on the west bank of the Lehigh River, East Allentown was the original site of the station. The station was located at Hamilton Street on the east bank of the River. This station was closed in 1890 with the opening of the new Allentown station. The station was razed in 1911.

Catasauqua
Catasauqua was eastablished as a station stop in 1867. The following year a combination (freight and passenger) station was constructed. This station was closed in 1893, but was still standing in 1918. In 1893 a new 19 x 83' one-story frame station was built. The 1893 station was demolished in 1955.

Northampton
Eastablished in 1867 with the name of Laubach's. The name was changed to Stemton around 1876 and renamed Northampton around 1896. A 18' x 66' one story frame conbination station was built in 1893. The station was closed in 1920 and razed in the 1970s.

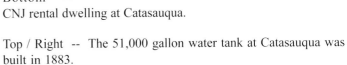

Top / Left / Top -- The Catasauqua station.

Top / Left / Bottom -- CNJ rental dwelling at Catasauqua.

Top / Right -- The 51,000 gallon water tank at Catasauqua was built in 1883.

Middle / Left -- Northampton station, circe 1960. Collection of William Krug.

Siegfried

Originally established as Siegfried's Bridge in 1867, the name was changed to Siegfried in the late 1870s. A 18' x 44' one-story frame station was built in 1888. In 1892, a new 20' x 51' one-story frame station was constructed, at which time the 1888 station was converted into a freight house. The station was closed during the depression and an old car body was used as shelter.

Bottom -- The 1888 Siegfried station can be seen behind the 1892 station.

Middle / Right -- The machine shop used by the bridge department at Siegfried.

Top / Left -- The sand house and bunk house was built at Siegfried in 1898. They were removed from the accountanting books in 1929 and officially abandoned in 1944.

Top / Right -- In 1871 an enclosed water tank was built at Treichler. The tank was expanded in 1873 and abandoned in 1952.

Middle / Top -- Treichler station. Collection of William Krug.

Treichler

With the construction of a station in 1867, Treichler was established as a station stop. Although the ticket office closed in 1952 with the discontinuence of passenger service, the freight agency remained opened until 1969.

Walnutport

The CNJ served passengers of Walnutport from 1867 to 1952. The 19' x 66' one-story frame combination station was officially retired in 1956. A turntable was built in 1867 and a water tank in 1871.

Middle / Bottom -- CNJ section grang #10 at the Walnutport station. The man wearing the overcoat is foreman Harry W. Stofs. Collection of James D. Brownback.

Bottom -- Walnutport station, circa 1950. Collection of William Krug.

Lehigh Gap

A combination 19' x 65' one-story frame station was built at Lehigh Gap shortly after it was established as a station in 1867. The station was discontinued in 1952. The station was then used as a road side food stand selling hot dogs, french fries and soda. The station was demolished in 1960.

Top -- Lehigh Gap station when it was being used a roadside food stand, circa 1955. Collection of William Krug.

Middle / Top -- Palmerton passenger and freight stations, circa 1939. Collection of James D. Brownback.

Middle / Bottom -- The Hazard station with freight station. The 16' x 19' freight station was built in 1888.

Palemerton

Unlike many of the other towns along this line which were established as a station stop by 1867, Palemerton was not established until February 8, 1911. Palemerton station was constructed due to the expansion of the New Jersey Zinc Company facilities at this location. The station was discontinued in 1952. This 22' x 80' one-story stone passenger station still stands today.

The 24' x 50' one-story frame Palemerton freight station was built in 1911 The freight station does not exist today.

Hazard

Established in 1880 as Hazardville, it was renamed to Hazard in 1884. Hazard was closed when the Palemerton station opened in 1911.

Bowmanstown

Originally established as Bowman's, the name was changed to Bowmanstown around 1900. The station was combination station built in the 1870s or early 1880s. The freight room was expanded in 1892. The station was demolished in 1965.

Bottom -- Bowmanstown station, circa 1945. Collection of William Krug.

Parryville

Established as a station in 1867, the Parryville station was opened in July, 1873. The station was a 17' x 47' one-story frame combination station. Parryville was discontinued as a station in 1956.

Top -- Parryville station. Collection of William Krug.

Weissport

Weissport was established as a station stop in 1867. The 18' x 81' one-story frame station was built in 1878. The station was discontinued in 1952 and demolished in the late 1970s.

Middle -- Weissport station.

Lehighton

The 18' x 47" one-story frame Lehighton station was built in 1867. In 1883 a freight room of 18' x 20' was added to the station. The station was closed in 1952 and demolished in 1960.

Bottom / Left -- CNJ section gang at Weissport, circe 1939.

Bottom / Right -- Lehighton station. Collection of William Krug.

86

Mauch Chunk - Jim Thorpe

Although established as a station stop in 1865, the first railroad station was built in 1869. The railroad quickly realized that a larger and more substanial station was needed. In 1873 plans for a new station were drawn. These plans were simular to the station built at Bethlehem. However, due to a reclining economy and lack of funds, a new station was not built until 1888-89. This station still stands today and is used a vistor center and a small museum.

In the mid-1950s Maunch Chunk was renamed Jim Thorpe after a famouse football player. The station was discontinued in June of 1965.

Top -- Mauch Chunk station.

Middle / Left -- The Mauch Chunk freight station was built in 1888 and demolished in 1966. The freight station was located just north of the passenger station.

Middle / Right -- The 20' x 41' frame ice house was built at Mauch Chunk in 1893.

Bottom -- This photograph depicts "D" dipatcher's office which was located just south of the station. The building was built in 1869 and may have served as a passenger station. The southern ends of the passenger canopies for the 1888-89 station can be seen in the left hand side of the photograph.

Top / Left -- The yard master's office.

Top / Right -- The stone sand house.

Middle -- The sand tank located next to the sand house.

Bottom / Left -- The 1909 water tower.

Bottom / Right -- The oil house was built in 1890.

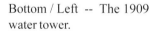

Top -- The freight car shops, built in 1888 were rebuilt in 1907-08. The shops had a capcity of eight cars within the building and sixty-nine in the repair yard. The boiler house for the car shops was built in 1889. Mississippi Central flat car #201 and a Pittsburg & Shawmut Railroad coal hopper can be seen in the photograph.

Middle / Top / Right -- The carpenter and blacksmith was built in 1907. The building burned in 1939.

Middle / Top / Left -- Rear view of the 1888 engine house at Mauch Chunk. The first engine facility was a 4 stall round house built in 1868. This was replaced with an 18 stall engine house. The engine house was located along the hill on the west side of the main line. Between 1938 and 1952 portions of the engine house were removed.

Middle / Bottom -- Another view of the freight car repair shops.

Bottom -- Lumber storage shed.

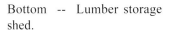

Drakes Point
Established as a flag stop between 1882-85 and abandoned by 1915.

Rockport
Rockport was established as a station stop in 1865. In 1888 a two-story combination station was constructed. By 1915 Rockport was a non-agency station. In 1901 a water tank was built next to the station. Rockport station was destroyed by the flooding caused by Hurricane Diane in August, 1955.

Top -- Rockport station. Collection of William Krug.

Leslie Run
A two-story combination station was built in 1872. The station was closed in 1919 by the United States Railroad Administration.

Drifton Junction
A Frank Furness designed station was built in 1884. The station burned on June 11, 1913. The station was never rebuilt and soon after Drifton Junction was discontinued as a station stop.

Maple Island
Was established as a flag stop in 1882 and abandoned in 1885

Tannery
A 17' x 24' one-story frame combination station was built in 1888. By 1915 the agency at Maple Island had been dissolved.

White Haven
Middle / Left -- The 19 x 110' one-story frame combination White Haven station. Collection of William Krug.

Middle / Right / Top & Bottom -- The first engine facilities were constructed at White Haven in 1848. In 1857 a new roundhouse and turntable were built. Three additional stalls were added to the roundhouse in 1860. A new stone roundhouse was built in 1866. This photograph depicts the remains of the 1866 roundhouse, circa 1915. One wall is a temporary wooden wall. The roundhouse was completely razed in 1925.

Bottom -- Signal store house.

Tunnel

Top -- Tunnel received its name from the 1,737' long railroad tunnel that was constructed at this location in the 1840s.

Top -- Tunnel station. Collection of William Krug.

Bergers, Crestwood and Glen Summit

All three of these station stops had small non-agency shelters.

Penobscot

Penobscot was established as a station stop around 1866. In 1888 a one-story frame combination station was constructed. The station was retired in 1959.

Solomon's Gap

In 1873 a 12' x 23' one-story frame station was built at the head of Ashley Planes. This station was named Solomon's Gap. By 1915 Solomon's Gap was a non-agency station.

Laurel Run

Laural Run station was built in 1874 and received an addition to the freight room in 1895. The station was removed in 1939.

Middle -- Laurel Run station.

Mountain Park

Established in 1883 as a stop for the CNJ owned and operated resort and amusement park. The park was closed in 1908 and the station was abandoned in 1911.

Bottom / Left -- "FQ" tower at Mountain Park was built in the 1890s and contained 20 levers. In 1907 a new machine was installed.

Ashley

Established in 1866 as Nanticoke Junction, the name was changed to Ashley in 1870. Ashley is located at the foot of the CNJ Ashley planes. In 1888 a 19' x 110' one-story frame station was built. In 1892 the freight room was extended.

Ashely was discontinued as a station stop on May 1, 1950, with the removal of the Scranton Flyer passenger train.

Page 91 / Bottom / Right -- Ashley station. Collection of William Krug.

Ashley Yards

In 1867 the repair facilities, maintained by the Lehigh & Sesquehanna Railroad (CNJ) at White Haven, were moved to Ashley and Ashley became the railroad's main shops in Pennsylvania. By 1920 the shops had a capacity to repair 15 steam locomotives, 50 cars in sheds and 173 cars in repair yards. The majority of work done at Ashley was the repair to coal hopper coals. In 1955 this work was transferred to the Elizabethport shops.

Top -- An overview of the Ashley yards, circa 1942. The 1910 4-track wooden coaling tower can be seen in the upper left corner. The roundhouse can be seen directly to the right of the water tower. Collection of James D. Brownback.

Middle / Left -- CNJ store house.

Middle / Right -- A diagram of the Ashley roundhouse, circa 1915. The old portion of the roundhouse was constructed in 1867-68. In 1910, 8 new stalls were added and two old stalls were lengthened. In 1944 the 8 shorter stalls of the original roundhouse were retired. The last steam engine to operate at Ashley was on January 12, 1952.

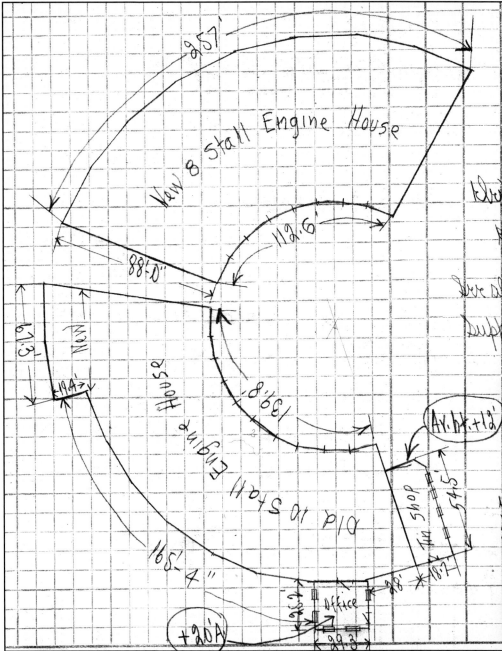

Top / Left / Top -- The oil house was a one-story brick building.

Top / Left / Bottom -- The carpenter shop was built in 1872. It was demolished in 1939.

Top / Right -- The original car shops were built in 1867. The shops were a 37' x 400' one-story frame building.

Middle / Top -- Another view of the original 1867 car shops.

Middle / Bottom -- In 1878 another car repair facility was built. This shop was a 97' x 300' frame building with 4 tracks extending the length of the building.

Bottom / Left -- The freight car paint shop was a 50' x 211' frame building built in 1868.

Bottom / Right -- The freight car paint shop stock room was built in 1891.

Top / Left -- Boiler shop at Ashley yard.

Top / Right / Top -- The original blacksmith shop was destroyed by fire on May 30, 1881. A new 46' x 88' one-story frame shop building was built in 1888.

Top / Right / Bottom -- This building housed the first aid center, the yard office, and the pattern shop office.

Middle -- The machine shop was built in 1868.

Bottom -- Another view of the 1868 machine shop which was leased to a scrap dealer in 1954.

South Wilkes-Barre

A 16' x 57' one-story frame combination station was constructed in 1890. The station was closed by the United States Railroad Administration (USRA) between 1918 and 1920.

Hazel Street, Wilkes-Barre

Established as a station stop in 1875 with the construction of a 16' x 53' one-story frame combination station. The station was closed by the USRA, circa 1919.

Wilkes-Barre

Established as a station stop in 1866, construction on the station began in 1867. The station was completed in August, 1868. Wilkes-Barre was discontinued as a station stop in July, 1963. The station was sold and converted into a restaurant and motel.

Top -- The Wilkes-Barre freight house was built 1868. In 1873 a 25' x 219' addition was added to the freight station. The freight station was once again expanded in 1909. The CNJ sold the freight station and it was used by a local feed store. The building was demolished in 1969.

Middle -- The Wilkes-Barre station.

Sheldon

Sheldon was a flagstop established in January of 1887. The station stop was discontinued by 1915.

Bottom -- Miners Mill station. Collection of William Krug.

Parsons

A combination station was built in 1872-73. The freight room was extended in 1890. The dimensions of the station in 1915 was 18' x 83'.

Miners Mills

Miners Mills was established as a station stop in 1872-73 with the construction of a combination station. The freight room was extended in 1898. In 1915 the dimensions of the station was 18' x 65'. The station agency was closed by the USRA in 1918-20.

Hudson

Eastablished in 1867 under the name of Mill Creek, the name was then changed to Hudson. The station was built in 1887 and removed before 1915.

Union Junction
Between Union Junction and Minooka Junction the CNJ traveled on the Delaware & Hudson Railroad (D&H).

Laflin, D&H

Yatesville, D&H

Pittston, D&H
Top -- Pittston Station. Collection of William Krug.

Avoca, D&H

Moosic, D&H
Middle / Top -- Moosic station was established in 1867 under the name Spring Brook. Collection of William Krug.

Minooka Junction

Taylor
In 1888 a one-story frame combination station was built at Taylor. The station was extended in 1902.

Middle / Bottom -- CNJ bridge 100 1/2 at Taylor.

Fifth Avenue, Scranton
By 1895 Fifth Avenue, in Scranton was established as a flagstop. The agency was abandoned by 1905, but the station remained on the non-agency station list for several more years.

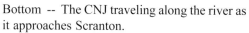

Bottom -- The CNJ traveling along the river as it approaches Scranton.

Scranton
Established in 1888 with the construction of an elaborate station on Lackawanna Avenue. The station opened on May 1, 1888. On December 18, 1910, the station was destroyed along with two coaches by fire. A temporary 20' x 57' one-story frame station was built nearby. The temporary station was never replaced and was used until passenger service was stopped on May 1, 1950. The New York, Ontario and Western also used the CNJ station between 1890 and 1930.

Top / Left -- The coaling tower at Scranton.

Top / Right -- The original ornate CNJ passenger station. The CNJ freight station can be seen to the right of the bridge. Collection of William Krug.

Middle -- Built after the fire destroyed the original Scranton station, this temporary building became the permanent CNJ station at Scranton.

Bottom / Left -- Approaching Scranton. The freight house can be seen in the background. The freight house was a two-story brick building built in 1890-91.

Bottom / Right -- Bridge 105 1/4. The second passenger station can be seen behind the bridge.

Views Around Scranton

CHAPTER 6

ASHLEY PLANES, PA

Top -- A view of the top of Ashley Plane #1.

Middle / Left -- Engine house for Plane #1.

Middle / Right -- Engine house for Ashley Plane #2.

Bottom -- Engine house for Plane #3.

Top / Left -- Water tank at Plane #2.

Top / Right -- Boiler house at Plane #3.

Bottom -- Office and water tower at Plane #3.

Top -- Old round-house being used as a store house in Ashley on the Nanticoke Branch.

Bottom -- The Wanamie station. Collection of William Krug.

Sugar Notch

A 14'x 21' one-story frame shelter was built at Sugar Notch in 1888. The station was discontinued prior to 1929 and officially retired in 1944.

Warrior Run

A 15' x 25' one-story frame combination station was built in 1872. The ICC listed this station in 1915 as having only a freight agency.

Auchincloss

Established under the name Hanover, this location was a non-agency station stop. A freight house was built in 1893.

Leemine

Leemine had a non-agency station or shelter.

Alden

In 1875 a one-story frame combination station was built. By 1915 the station was listed as a non-agency station. On June 4, 1940, the station was destroyed by fire. The CNJ removed the 1882 freight house that same year.

Wanamie

Established in 1867 under the name Newport. Passenger service began to this station in 1868. A two-story combination station was built shortly thereafter. In 1872 a one-story addititon to the freight room was added. A water tower was built in 1871. Both the station and water tower were retired in 1955.

Lee

Lee was a non-agency station. A freight house was built in 1889.

Top / Left -- Old box cars bodies being used as bunk houses at Nesquehoning Junction.

Top / Right -- Nesquehoning station. Collection of William Krug.

Middle / Right -- Hauto station was a 12' x 17' one-story frame non-agency station. Collection of William Krug.

Middle / left -- The second bridge to cross the Little Schuylkill River at Hometown was built in 1896. The bridge is 987' long and 175' high. It replaced the original 1869 wooden bridge.

Bottom -- The renewal of the Hometown bridge in 1931 by Phoenix Bridge Co. cost $208,800. Collection of James D. Brownback.

Top -- The 1893 westbound station at Pacific Avenue.

Pacific Avenue

Leaving the CNJ main Line at Communipaw, the Newark Branch traveled trough Jersey City to Newark. The first station, Pacific Avenue was only .4 of a mile away from Communipaw.

Pacific Avenue was established as a station stop in the late 1860s or early 1870s under the name of Lafayette. Between 1878 and 1881 a station was constructed at this site. A 17' x 37' one-story frame westbound station was built in 1893.

Just west of the Pacific Avenue station, the CNJ Lafayette Branch bears off the Newark Branch and travels along the east side of the Morris Canal. This branch served several industries, but also had a non-agency station at Griffings.

Arlington Avenue

In 1887-89 a station was constructed on the westbound side. In 1910 a one-story stone station was built on the eastbound side.

Middle -- The 1910 eastbound station at Arlington Avenue.

Jackson Avenue

Established in 1869 under the name of Bergen Avenue. The station was located just east of Bergen Avenue. In 1877 a new frame station was constructed on the east side of Jackson Avenue. At which time the Bergen Avenue station was closed. This station was replaced in 1892.

A two-story white brick station opened on the west side of Jackson Avenue on March 20, 1911. The passenger platforms were located in Bergen Hill cut and were reached by stairs and an elevator.

This station was also used by the Lehigh Valley Railroad between 1913 and 1918. The station closed in 1948 and was sold in 1951. It was converted into a furniture store and later a storefront church.

Bottom -- Jackson Avenue station.

West Side Avenue

Established in 1869 as West Bergen, the station was located west of Mallory Street. In the late 1870s a new station was built at West Side Avenue. In 1887-88 a new two-story brick westbound station was constructed. In 1910 a 15' x 40' one-story brick eastbound station was built.

Top -- The 1887-88 brick westbound West Side Avenue station.

Middle / Top / Left -- The 1910 eastbound station at West Side Avenue.

Hackensack River Drawbridge

The first bridge was constructed in 1867-69. This bridge has a swing draw with 50' clearance on either side. A new 212' draw span bridge was built in 1888.

On August 11, 1913 the American Bridge Company began construction on replacing the 1888 bridge. The track was raised 22'. The new bridge was of a swing draw design. The bridge opened on October 5, 1913.

On Febuary 3, 1946 the collier *Jagger Seam* hit the bridge knocking two spans into the water. The bridge was never rebuilt.

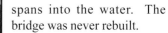

Middle / Bottom / Left -- The Hackensack River drawbridge.

Middle / Right -- The center of the swing of the 1913 bridge. This 11 lever cabin replaced two smaller 5 lever cabins that were at each end of the bridge.

Bottom -- A rare photograph of a CNJ rowboat.

Passaic River Drawbridge

In the 1860s a swing drawbridge was constructed with a 90' clearance on either side. In 1888 the draw was rebuilt to a 172' span. The American Bridge Company replaced the bridge in the fall of 1913. At this time the track was elevated 22', eliminating 90% of the openings.

In 1908 5 lever interlocking cabins were built on both ends of the bridge. With the opening of the new 1913 bridge, one interlocking cabin on the west end of the bridge replaced the two smaller cabins. This cabin was a 8' x 40' one-story frame building with 23 levers.

Newark Transfer

Established on December 21, 1913, as a station for passengers to transfer to trains using the Brills Branch. A 13' x 200' one-story station was constructed in 1916. The station stop was abolished on April 30, 1967.

East Brills

East Brills station served as transfer station for Lehigh Valley Railroad passengers to transfer to CNJ Newark bound trains. The station was a small shelter and was only used between 1892 and 1893. In November of 1893 LV trains resumed their passenger route over the Pennsylvania Railroad (PRR) to Jersey City.

Top -- Newark Transfer. Collection of William Krug.

Middle -- "BT" tower at Brills Junction was built in 1913-14. The tower was a 15' x 30' two-story red brick building with 29 levers.

Bottom / Right -- Bridge #200 over the PRR was built in 1902 by the American Bridge Company and the Phoenix Bridge Company.

East Ferry Street, Newark

East Ferry Street was established as a station stop in 1869. The first station was a long frame building. A new station was built between 1878 and 1881. In November of 1911 the third station was opened at this location. The station was a two-story brick building which had the appearance of regular commercial building. The station was retired in 1953 and demolished in the 1970s.

Bottom / Left -- The East Ferry Street station. The metal passenger canopies can be seen behind the building.

Top -- The freight house near East Ferry Street station was built in 1917 on St. Charles Street. The freight house was a 25' x 157' one-story frame building. The freight house was retired in 1951 and sold to P.Ballentine & Sons Brewery in 1954.

Ferry Street, Newark

Established as a station stop in 1869 an impressive three-story brick station was built in 1871-72. The first floor housed commercial businesses. The waiting room was located on the second floor. The third floor and mansard roof were removed at one point. The station closed on April 30, 1967.

Middle -- Ferry Street Station.

Bottom -- "NA" tower at Mulberry Street was built in 1902. The elevated frame building was 15' x 33' and contained 52 levers. It was retired in 1962 and demolished in 1964.

Broad Street, Newark

On July 23, 1869, the first station opened, establishing Broad Street as a station stop. The station was a freight - passenger combination station. Between 1878 and 1881 the station was enlarged and a separate freight house was built on Fair Street. There was a wooden train shed covering four tracks. The station was renovated in 1899.

Near the Broad Street station the CNJ interchanged with the Pennsylvania Railroad. The interchange track was at a 3% grade. In 1901 the Pennsylvania Railroad began to elevate their track forcing the CNJ to raise their track to keep the grade of the interchange track to a minium. It also allowed the CNJ to eliminate the at-grade crossing of Mulberry Street. In April of 1901 construction began on the raising of the tracks and a new train shed. In 1902 construction began on a new station.

Construction began on the third station at this location around 1916. The new station was a two-story brick building with a 60' frontage on Broad Street. The rear of the station was 266' wide with a 66' x 166' concourse with the capacity to hold 2,000 people. The CNJ needed the large capacity to accommodate the excursion trains. A 4 track concrete bush style train shed was built ranging from 86' to 400' long. The longest platform was 1040'. The station was abandoned on April 29, 1967, and the track was removed from the train shed in 1968. During the switchman strike in May, 1971, passenger trains returned to the station for two days. The train shed was demolished in 1985 and the station was sold and converted into a mall in 1986.

CHAPTER 10

NEWARK & ELIZABETH BRANCH, NJ

Brills Junction
Brills Junction is the point that the Newark & Elizabeth Branch left the Newark Branch. A tower controlled the juction. (see page 105) The CNJ maintained a freight yard at Brills Junction which included an automobile unloading facility and a car shop for repairing coal cars.

Top -- Brills yard master's office was a 18' x 36' two-story building.

South Brills
A non-agency freight station was located at South Brills. South Brills was never a passenger station stop.

Hamburg Place
Hamburg Place had a non-agency freight station.

Oak Island Junction
The Pennsylvania Railroad and the Lehigh Valley Railroad crossed the CNJ at Oak Island Junction. The PRR crossed extended their line across the CNJ in 1901 and the LV in 1913.

In 1903 "CY" tower was built to control the crossover. The tower contained 44 levers. On Febuary 27, 1913 a new "CY" tower was opened. This tower was a two-story brick tower which was jointly owned between the three railroads. The CNJ owned 39.4%, the PRR owned 16.7% and the LV owned 43.9%.

Middle -- "CY" tower.

Newark Airport
Established as Port Newark the name was later changed to Newark Airport. A small shelter was constructed at this location. Newark Airport was abolished on April 30, 1967.

Bottom -- Newark Airport shelter. Collection of William Krug.

Great Island Juction
The Newark & Elizabeth branch junctioned with the ELizabeth Extension Branch at this location.

Top / Left -- Looking northwest along Broadway from Third Street.

Top / Right -- Looking northwest along Broadway from Fourth Street.

Middle / Left -- Looking southwest along Broadway from Fourth Street.

Middle / Right -- Looking southwest along Broadway from Fifth Street.

Bottom / Right -- Looking southwest along Broadway from New Point Road.

Bottom / Left -- Crossing tower at First Street & Port Avenue.

Top / Left -- Scale house at Second Street.

Top / Right -- Elizabethport Docks yard master's office.

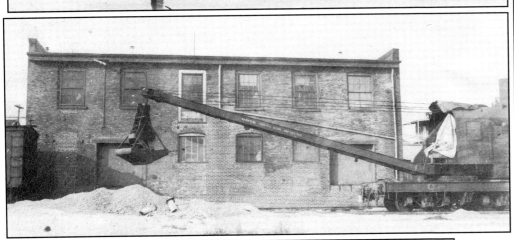

Middle / Top / Left -- Passenger station at Fourth Street & Port Avenue.

Middle / Top / Right -- Freight storehouse at Elizabethport Docks.

Middle / Bottom / Left -- Freight house at Elizabethport Docks.

Middle / Bottom / Right -- Coal offices at Elizabethport Docks.

Bottom -- Pier #6 was built in 1906. The pier was a 3 track gravity pier which was retired in 1935.

Roycefield

Eastablished as a station stop in 1866 under the name of Ricefield. A 9' x 31' one-story frame non-agency station was constructed in 1903. The station was retired in 1955.

Flagtown

The Flagtown combination station was built in 1888. The station was a 20' x 40' one-story frame building. The station building was sold in 1953.

Top -- The passenger and freight combination station at Flagtown.

Neshanic

A CNJ standard station was built at Neshamic in 1864, establishing this location as a station stop. In 1903 a 20' x 40' one-story frame freight station was built.

Middle -- Neshanic station.

Woodfern

By 1915 the station at Woodfern was a non-agency staton. The station was a 14' x 23' one-story frame building.

Bottom / Left -- Woodfern station. Collection of William Krug.

Higgin's Mill

Established as Riverside the name was changed to Higginsville and then again to Higgin's Mill. The 13' x 17' one-story frame station was built in 1903. The station was retired in 1951.

Page 110 / Bottom / Right -- Higgin's Mill station. Collection of William Krug.

Three Bridges

Established as a station stop in 1864, a CNJ standard station was built soon afterwards. The station was demolished and the ground sold to New Jersey Power & Light in 1955. A 20' x 40' one-story frame freight house was built in 1864.

Top -- Three Bridges station.

Middle / Right -- The water tank at Flemington was retired in 1954.

Middle / Left -- The South Branch crosses the South Branch Raritan River several times. The original 1863-64 wooden bridge at this location was built by J.K. Large. This bridge was rebuilt in 1885. The Phoenix Bridge Company replaced the wooden span in 1897.

Flemington

Established as a station stop in 1864, a CNJ standard station was constructed one year later. In 1953 the station was sold to Flemington Cut Glass Company. In the 1960s the station was converted into a restaurant.

Bottom / Left -- The Flemington station.

Bottom / Right -- In 1903 a 39' x 65' 2 stall engine house was built at Flemington. The engine house was retired in 1935. A 65' turntable and ash pits were also built at this location.

111

Hoffmans

Hoffmans was established prior to 1892 under the name of Hoffman's Siding. A 10' x 14' one-story frame non-agency station was built in 1898.

George Bridge

The CNJ crossed over the South Branch Raritan River several times, one of which was at this location. The first bridge, built in 1876, was a wooden trestle which collapsed under the weight of an ore train on April 18, 1885. The bridge was quickly rebuilt and reopened on April 24, 1885. The bridge was once again replaced in 1891.

Califon

Califon was established as a station stop in 1876. A one-story stone station was built in 1893. A 17' x 28' one-story frame freight house was constructed in 1883.

Top -- The Califon station. Collection of William Krug.

Vernoy

A 10' x 19' one story frame non-agency station was built near the end of the nineteenth century.

Crestmoor

On June 27, 1897 Crestmoor was established as a station stop. The 5' x 13' one story frame non-agency station was opened in 1989. The station was retired in 1935.

Middle Valley

In 1876 one-story frame station was constructed establishing Middle Valley as a station stop. In 1903 8' x 10' one-story frame freight shelter shed was built.

Long Valley

Originally established as German Valley in 1876, the name was changed to Long Valley due to the anti-German sediment during World War I. The one-story frame station was built in 1888.

Middle -- German Valley station.

Bottom -- The CNJ maintained a scale and water tank at Long Valley. The water tower was built in 1916. The scale was retired in 1945.

Naughright

Naughright station was built in 1876 establishing it as a station stop. The station was closed in the early 1900s and removed. A 8' x 12' one-story frame non-agency station was built in 1910.

Bartley

Established in 1876, Bartley station was built that same year. In 1898 a 14' x 40' one-story frame station replaced the original station.

Top -- Bartley Station. Collection of William Krug.

Middle -- Bridge #260 over the South Branch Raritan River was located at mile marker 14 between Naughright and Bartley. The original 1875 bridge was rebuilt by Cofrade & Saylor in 1891.

Flanders

Flanders was established as a station stop in 1876. The 17' x 40' one-story frame station was built between 1876 and 1878.

Bottom -- Flanders station. Collection of William Krug.

Cary's

Established as a station stop with the construction of a station in 1876. The station was updated in 1893. The station was a 12' x 16' one-story frame non-agency station.

Ledgewwod

Drakesville station stop was established in 1876. The name was later changed to Ledgewood. In 1888 a 16' x 35' one-story frame station was constructed.

Top -- Bridge #262 over Drake's Brook near Ledgewood. The original bridge was built in 1875. This photograph depicts the bridge after it was rebuilt in 1909.

Kenvil

Kenvil was established as a station stop in 1876. A 26' x 34' one-story frame station was built in 1887. The station was destroyed by fire in January, 1972.

Middle -- Kenvil station.

Ferromont Junction

Ferromont Junction was the point where the High Bridge Branch crossed the DL&W's Chester Branch. The narrow gauge Ferromonte Railroad also connected at this point between 1870 and 1872.

An 9' x 9' one-story frame interlocking cabin with 5 levers was built in 1903.

Hopatcong Junction

Hopatcong Junction was the junction of the High Bridge Branch and the Lake Hopatcong Branch of the CNJ. The 16' x 26' one-story frame station was built in 1889-1892. By 1915 the station was listed as a non-agency station.

Bottom -- Bridge #273 over the DL&W tracks at Wharton was built in 1889.

Bottom / Left -- Hopatcong Junction station.

Wharton

With the construction of a station in 1876, Port Oram was established as a station stop. The station was a 18' x 51' one-story frame building. The name was changed to Wharton between 1892 and 1900.

Top -- Bridge #272 over the Morris Canal at Wharton. The bridge was built by Cofrade & Saylor in 1895.

Dover

Dover was established as a station stop in the early 1880s. The three-story frame passenger station was constructed in 1883. The station was converted to a commercial building in 1934.

A 22' x 85' one-story freight house was built in 1898. The freight house was sold in 1963.

It is interesting to note that the CNJ crossed the Morris Canal at Dover by means of a draw bridge. In 1909 an interlocking cabin with 5 levers was built at the draw bridge.

Middle -- The Dover passenger station. The station sign can barely be seen on the right side of the photograph.

Dover Driving Park

Dover Driving Park station on June 27, 1897. The station was abandoned less then twenty years later in 1916.

Hiberina Junction

A non-agency freight station was located at this junction between the DL&W and the CNJ.

Rockaway

The first station built at Rockaway was in 1887. This station was replaced with a one-story frame station built in 1905. The CNJ maintained an engine terminal consisting of an engine house, coal stockade and water tanks at Rockaway.

Bottom -- Rockaway station. Collection of William Krug.

Stickle Avenue

On June 27, 1897 the Stickle Avenue station opened.

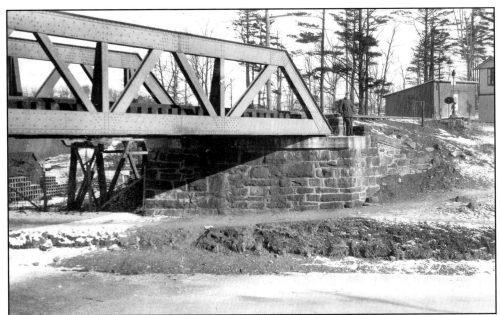

Hibernia

The Beach Glen Mine and several other owned by the Andover Iron Company were located around Hibernia. The tracks to Hibernia were abandoned in 1943. No information is available on the Hibernia station.

Lake Junction

Just six tenths of a mile away from Hopatcong Junction the CNJ junctioned with the DL&W. This junction became known as Lake Junction. In 1913 the CNJ and the DL&W constructed a 9' x 9' one-story frame interlocking cabin with 5 levers at the junction. The cabin was jointly owned at 50% each.

The CNJ built a one-story frame station at Lake Junction in 1893. The station was most likely a small shelter.

Morris County Junction

The Morris County Railroad, also known as the Wharton & Northern, junctioned with the CNJ at this location. A small one-story frame station served the junction.

Top -- The small shelter station at Espanong can be seen underneath bridge #301. Espanong Road bridge was built in 1889.

Bottom -- CNJ dwelling, originally Nolan's Point Villa, at Lake Hopatcong.

Minisink

In 1894 the Minisink station was only open on Sundays. A new station was built in 1902. The station was a small one-story frame station. By 1915 Minisink was listed as a non-agency station.

Espanong

The 7' x 16' one-story frame shelter was built under Espanong Road in Espanong in 1898.

Lake Hopatcong

In 1888, a 22' x 33' one-story frame station was built. In 1890 the CNJ purchase a large amount of land at Nolan's Point, Lake Hopatcong to develop an excursion location. A 8' x 50' one-story shelter was built along with a large Villa. The CNJ charged $2.00 per day to stay at the Villa. The Villa later became rental dwellings.

Hurd

A shelter was built at Hurd to serve the Hurd Mine employees.

Weldon

A shelter was built at Weldon to serve the Magie Mine and the Upper and Lower Weldon Mines.

Ford

A shelter was built to serve the employees of the Ford Mine.

Mahola

Top -- The Mahola shelter was retired in 1934. Collection of William Krug.

Edison

Established as Ogden the name was changed to Edison after Thomas A. Edison purchased a mine at this location to conduct his experiments of separating iron ore electromagnetically.

CHAPTER 15
CHESTER BRANCH, LONG VALLEY TO CHESTER, NJ

Bottom / Left -- Bridge #290 over the South Branch Raritan River was built in 1901.

Chester

Chester was established as a station stop in 1876. A 16' x 28' one-story frame combination station was built in 1888.

Bottom / Right -- Chester station. Collection of William Krug.

Morses Creek
In 1898, an 8' x 8' one-story frame non-agency shelter station was built at Morses Creek. This station stop was abolished in 1960.

Grasselli
A 19' x 79' one-story frame station was constructed at Grasselli. The station was used until 1959.

Top -- Grasselli station. Collection of William Krug.

Tremley Point
A passenger platform was the only improvement made to this station stop.

Warners
A 10' x 20' one story frame non-agency shelter station was built in 1898. The shelter was abandoned in 1960.

Middle -- Warners station. Collection of William Krug.

Williams & Clark Chemical
In 1898, a 10' x 20' one-story frame non-agency shelter station was constructed. The shelter was retired in 1934 and the station stop abolished in April, 1959.

Carteret
A 26' x 64' one-story frame station was built in 1902. Carteret was abandoned as a passenger stop in 1959.

Page 119 / Top -- Carteret station. Collection of William Krug.

Liebigs Lane
Originally established as Canda in respect to the Canda family which bought the Chrome Steel Works in 1895. A non-agency frame shelter served passengers at this location. The name was changed to Liebigs Lane after the name of the street on which the shelter was located.

Bottom -- Liebigs Lane shelter. Collection of William Krug.

Chrome
Originally established as Sawyer's, the name was changed to Chrome by 1915. In 1898, a 12' x 31' one-story frame station was built. The station was retired in 1956 and was discontinued as a passenger stop in 1959.

Bottom -- Chrome station. Collection of William Krug.

Elizabethport

Historical information for this station can be found on page 52.

Top -- The standard CNJ station at Elizabethport.

Elizabeth Avenue, Elizabethport

Established as a station stop in 1875. New eastbound and westbound stations were constructed during the track elevation project of 1910-12. The stations opened on December 1, 1912. The eastbound station was a 31' x 71 one-story brick station. The westbound station was a one-story brick building and was retired in 1937. The westbound station was demolished to permit the widening of the New Jersey Turnpike.

Bayway

In 1884, a replacement station was built at Bayway. A 13' x 27' one-story frame non-agency shelter station was built in 1908. The station was demolished in 1953.

Middle -- Bayway station. Collection of William Krug.

Tremley

Established as a station stop in 1875, the station was built in 1883. The station was a 21' x 41' two-story frame building. By 1915 it was a non-agencye station and was being rented as a dwelling.

West Carteret

East Rahway was established as a station stop in 1875. The name was changed to West Carteret between 1922 and 1924. The station was built in 1888 and was in a simular design to the station at Spingtown, NJ. The station was a 21' x 43' two-story frame building. By 1915 the station was being rented out as a dwelling.

Bottom -- West Carteret station, circa 1915, when the station sign still read "East Rahway."

West Chrome

West Chrome station was built in 1913. The station was a 15' x 26' one-story frame station with a passenger canopy directly in front of the station. The station became a non-agency station in 1924.

Top -- West Chrome station.

Port Reading

In 1903, a 14' x 17' one-story frame station with a passenger canopy was constructed at Port Reading. Port Reading was also known as Port Reading Crossing. The station was demolished during a highway overpass project.

The Reading Railroad maintained a rail yard and coal docks at Port Reading. Port Reading was home to a joint CNJ and Reading Railroad creosote plant which prepared all of the wooden ties for both railroads.

Middle -- The station at Port Reading Crossing.

Bottom / Right -- "PD" tower at Port Reading was joint owned. The CNJ owned 16.3% while the Reading owned 83.7%. The original 15' x 15' 1893 tower was rebuilt in 1904. The tower was again rebuilt in 1907. In 1924 the 12 mechanical levers were replaced with a 10 lever electric machine. The tower was closed in 1963 and the control of the interlockings was moved to "RH" tower in West Carteret.

Sewaren

Established in 1875 as Woodbridge, it was renamed Sewaren in 1881. The 21' x 51' two-story station was built in 1883. The station was a standard CNJ station plan with the addition of an attic. The station was destroyed by fire on August 3, 1957. In 1959 a passenger shelter was constructed. Sewaren was abolished as a station stop on April 30, 1967 and the passenger shelter was removed in 1968.

Page 121 / Bottom / Left -- The embellished CNJ standard station at Sewaren.

Top -- Just north of the station, the Sewaren freight station was built in 1883.

Middle / Left -- The 25' x 40' one-story freight house was built at Maurer (Barber) in 1911.

Middle / Right-- Crossing tower near Sewaren.

Boynton Beach

Established to serve the beach and amusement grounds on Arthur Kill prior to 1905. The station was listed as a non-agency station on the CNJ 1915 station list. Industrial pollution closed the beach area and the station stop was abolished by 1924.

Barber

Established as Maurer's in honor of the Henry Maurer Asphalt Company, the name was changed to Barber on January 1, 1938. The name change was due to the name change of the asphalt company.

The station was a large two-story brick station built in 1894. Two wings were added in 1938.

Bottom -- Maurer station.

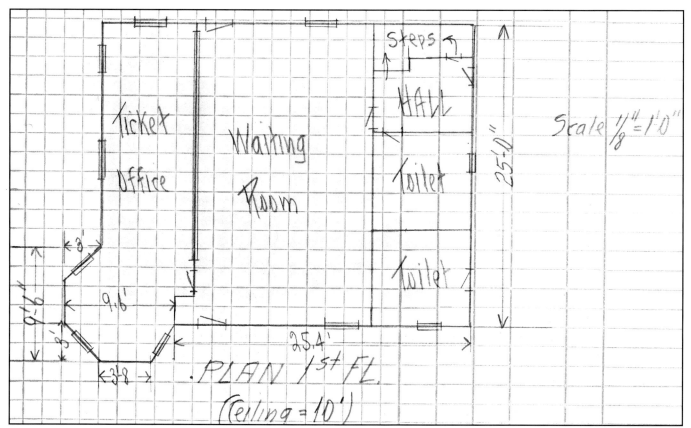

Top -- A diagram of the first floor layout of Maurer's station.

Middle -- "WO" tower opened on December 12, 1912. The tower was 14' x 30' and contained 29 levers. The tower was destroyed by fire in July, 1965.

Perth Amboy

Established as a station stop in 1875, the station was built soon afterwards. The station was a standard CNJ station with the embellished attic. In 1922 the CNJ began a grade crossing elimination project. The CNJ depressed their track from Hall Avenue to Market Street. The project was completed on June 29, 1928, with the completion of a new eastbound and westbound station. The total cost of the project was $2,152,342. During this project the original station was demolished.

Bottom -- The original CNJ embellished standard station at Perth Amboy. The small building to the right of the station is a baggage room which was built in 1896. The baggage building was a 10' x 19' frame building.

Top -- In 1896 the original 1876 freight station was replaced with a long 23' x 267' one-story frame freight station. The freight station was destroyed by fire in the late 1960s.

Middle -- Another view of the Perth Amboy freight house. The station can be seen in the distance.

Bottom -- CNJ bunk house at Perth Amboy. Two watch towers can also be seen in the photograph.

Raritan River Drawbridge

Top / Right -- From Perth Amboy, the line crossed the Raritan River Drawbridge into South Amboy.

South Amboy

Top / Left -- The CNJ maintained water tanks at South Amboy.

Morgan

Middle / Left -- The small one-story frame shelter station at Morgan.

Matawan
A slightly altered CNJ standard station was consturcted in 1875. In 1982-83 this station was replaced with a new station.

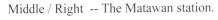
Middle / Right -- The Matawan station.

Matawan Junction
Matawan Junction was originally established in 1877 under the name of Freehold Junction. This was the point at which the Freehold branch met the Seashore branch. A platform was constructed. This station stop was discontinued in 1890.

Brown's Point Lane
Discontinued in 1880, just three years after it was established as a station stop in 1877.

Keyport
Keyport was established as a station stop in 1879. A one-story station was built in 1890. The station burned in 1968.

Bottom -- The one-story frame freight station at Keyport.

Top -- Keyport station.

First Street, Keyport

Established as a station stop with the construction of a station in 1880. Passenger usage never materialized and the station stop was discontinued in 1884. The station was demolished in 1907.

In 1885 a freight house was built. This freight house was replaced in 1902. The 1902 freight house was demolished in September, 1974.

Union Beach

Around 1921 Union Beach was established as a station stop. The station was destroyed by fire in 1958 and replaced with a shelter. Union Beach station was discontinued in 1966.

Natco

Originally established in 1880 under the name of Lorillard, the name was changed to Natco during the late 1910s. A one-story frame passenger shelter was built in 1901. With the opening of Union Beach station, Natco became a flag stop. Soon afterwards Natco was discontinued as a station stop all together. It was removed from the railroad accounting books in May, 1935.

Keansburg

Established as a station stop in 1889, a one-story frame station was built in 1891. In 1911 the station was enlarged with the addition of a passenger canopy and a baggage room. The station was sold in 1964 and demolished in the early 1970s.

Middle / Right -- The building on the right is the baggage room which was connected to the Keansburg station by a passenger canopy.

Port Monmouth

Established as a station stop with the construction of a station in 1889. This station was moved to Belford in December, 1890. A new one-story frame station similar to the Keansburg station was constructed in 1891. The CNJ sold the station in 1960 and it still stands today.

Middle / Left -- The 1891 Port Monmouth station. Collection of William Krug.

Belford

Port Monmouth Junction was established as a station stop in 1889. The one year old Port Monmouth station was moved to this location in December, 1890. The station was destroyed by fire in 1973.

Bottom -- The original Port Monmouth station at Belford.

Leonardo

Originally established under the name of Leonardo Avenue in 1891, the name was changed to Leonardo in the early twentieth century. A one-story frame station was built in 1900. The station was razed and replaced with a shelter shed in 1963. Leonardo was discontinued as a station stop in 1966.

Top -- Leonardo station.

Atlantic Highlands

Atlantic Highlands station was built in 1883. This station was converted into a freight house in 1890 at which time a temporary shed and platform was constructed. A new station was built in 1893. This station was destroyed by fire on December 16, 1951. A new station was built and opened on December 21, 1952. This station was demolished in 1973.

Bottom / Left -- Atlantic Highland station.

Bottom / Right -- CNJ pump house at Atlantic Highland.

Middle / Top -- The CNJ maintained an ice house at Atlantic Highlands.

Middle / Bottom -- The original station after it was converted into a freight house. The freight house was sold in 1959.

Atlantic Highlands Pier

In 1891-1892 the CNJ built a spur off of the Seashore branch into the Atlantic Ocean. This pier was opened on May 29, 1892. The CNJ used this pier for the Sandy Hook route ships. On September 14, 1944, the pier was damaged by a hurricane. The pier was retired in October, 1945 and the tracks and head house were removed in 1947. The pier burned on July 4, 1960, and again on May 6, 1966.

Bay View Avenue, Atlantic Highlands

A passenger station with a long canopy was built in 1892. A series of steps was constructed above the station to allow passengers to descend to track level. Bay View Avenue was discontinued as a station stop in 1941.

Top / Left -- In 1911 the CNJ built a bunk house at Atlantic Highlands. The bunk house was retired in 1943.

Top / Right -- Pier building leased to the Sandy Hook Yacht Club.

Middle / Top -- Atlantic Highlands Pier station.

Middle / Bottom -- A view of the steps leading down to track level at Bay View Avenue. The station was located directly beneath the steps.

Bottom / Left -- The remains of the steps and passenger canopy at Bay View Avenue station, circa 1940. Collection of William Krug.

Bottom / Right -- Hiltons passenger shelter station.

Hiltons

With the construction of a small one-story frame passenger shelter, Hiltons was established in 1896. Hilton was discontinued as a station stop in 1958.

Sandy Side

A one-story frame passenger shelter and platform was constructed at Sandy Side in 1895. Due to lack of usage the station stop was discontinued seven years later in 1902.

Water Witch

Water Witch was established as a station stop in 1895. A one-story brick station was constructed in 1903. In 1958 the station stop was discontinued and the station was demolished soon afterward.

Top / Left -- Water Witch station and newsstand.

Highlands

Originally established in 1892 under the name Highlands of Navesink, the name was changed to Highlands shortly after the turn of the century. A frame station was built in 1900. This station was replaced with a passenger shelter and platform around 1951.

Top / Right and Middle / Left -- Two views of the Highlands station.

Highland Beach

Established in 1866, Highland Beach went through several different name changes until Highland Beach was finally agreed upon in 1888. Prior to 1888 this station stop's name switched frequently between the names of Highlands of Navesink and Highlands. The first station to be constructed at this location was in 1874. This station was replaced with an ornate two-story frame station in 1892. The station was retired in 1944 and a small frame passenger shelter was constructed. Highland Beach was discontinued as a passenger stop in 1945.

Middle / Right -- The ornate 1892 two-story frame Highland Beach station.

Navesink Beach

A one-story frame passenger shelter was constructed in 1882, established Navesink Beach as a station stop. This shelter was replaced in 1912. Navesink Beach was discontinued as a passenger stop in 1945.

Normandie

Established as station stop in 1884 under the name of Bellevue. The name was changed to Normandie in 1888. In 1884 a very embellished, possibly a Frank Furness design, one-story frame station was built. This station was replaced with a shelter in the late 1910s.

Top -- The station at Normandie.

Middle / Top / Left -- The passenger shelter shed at Normandie.

Rumson Beach

Stokem's was established as a station stop in 1883. The name was changed to Rumson Beach in 1888. This station stop was discontinued around the turn of the century.

Laidlaws

Although not an official passenger stop, prior to 1902 passenger trains would stop at this location during the summer months. In 1902 the railroad built a platform and established Laidlaws as a regular summer stop. This station stop was discontinued in 1941.

Middle / Top / Right -- Sea Bright station.

Bottom -- Low Moor station.

Sea Bright

Established as station stop in 1866 under the name of Jumping Point. In 1867 the name was changed to Rumson's and in 1870 to Sea Bright. A one-story frame station was built in 1871. This station was replaced with a one-story brick station in 1900. The station was demolished in the early 1950s.

Middle / Bottom -- In 1899 a freight house was built to replace the original 1871 freight house.

Low Moor

Originally established as Monmouth Beach North in 1877, the name was changed to Low Moor in 1882. A one-story frame station was built in 1886. The station was removed in July, 1938.

Galilee

Established as station stop in 1877, under the name of Monmouth Beach Centre, renamed Monmouth Beach in 1882 and renamed Galilee in 1887. The original station was replaced with a one-story frame station in 1903. Galilee was abandoned as a station stop in 1942.

Top -- Galilee station.

Monmouth Beach

Established as station stop in 1877 under the name of Monmouth Beach South. The name was changed to Monmouth Beach in 1887. The original station was replaced in 1888 with a one-story stone building. This station was demolished in 1955.

Middle / Top -- Track side view of Monmouth Beach station.

Middle / Bottom -- Rear view of Monmouth Beach station.

North Long Branch

Atlanticville was established as a station stop in 1866. The name was changed to North Long Branch in 1881. The 1874 station was destroyed by fire on November 11, 1904. A one-story frame station was built in 1907. North Long Branch was discontinued as a station stop in 1945. The station was sold in 1952 and demolished in 1980.

Bottom -- Two views of the North Long Branch station. Collection of William Krug.

East Long Branch

In 1870 a one-story frame station was constructed, combining the stations of the Raritan & Delaware Bay (R&DB) and the Long Branch & Sea Shore Railroads (LB&SS). The R&DB station was built in 1864 and the LB&SS station was built in 1865.

East Long Branch was discontinued as a station stop in 1945 and the 1870 station was sold in 1946. The station was demolished in the late 1960s.

Top / Left -- Track side view of the East Long Branch station.

Top / Right -- In 1876 an office building was constructed at East Long Branch. The offices closed in 1930 and the building was retired in 1935.

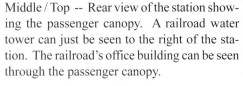

Middle / Top -- Rear view of the station showing the passenger canopy. A railroad water tower can just be seen to the right of the station. The railroad's office building can be seen through the passenger canopy.

Middle / Bottom -- The watch box, water tank and house, and coal box at East Long Branch.

Bottom -- In 1870 a roundhouse and turntable was built at East Long Branch. The roundhouse was closed in 1945 and demolished in 1947.

Rockwell Avenue, Branchport
Established as flag stop in 1912, it was discontinued in 1930.

Branchport
In 1876 a two-story frame modified CNJ standard station was constructed at Branchport. In 1930 a northbound passenger shelter was constructed. The station was discontinued on June 8, 1955. In 1956 the station was destroyed by fire.

Top -- The modified CNJ standard station at Branchport.

Middle / Left -- The water tank at Branchport.

Middle / Right -- The baggage room at the Branchport station.

Bottom / Right -- Branchport's freight house.

Oceanport
Oceanport was established as a station stop in 1860. A small one-story frame station was constructed in 1861. The station was demolished in the 1930s.

Bottom / Left -- Oceanport station.

Main Street, Eatontown
Established as a station stop in 1860, Main Street, Eatontown station was closed in 1872 when the agency was moved to the new Eatontown station.

Long Branch

Top / Left and Top / Right -- Two views of the two-story frame station at Long Branch.

Middle / Left -- An interior view of the railroad's office building at Long Branch.

Middle / Right -- An exterior view of the railroad's office.

Bottom / Left -- Coal trestle and recoaling facilities at Long Branch.

Bottom / Right -- A three stall engine house was part of the engine facilities the CNJ maintained at this location.

Top / Left -- Water tower at Long Branch. The building in the foreground is the railroad's three stall engine house.

West End

West End station was built in 1889. The station was a unique two-story frame building. The station was destroyed by fire on August 27, 1921. A new station was constructed in 1922. The station was closed on June 8, 1955.

Top / Right, Middle and Bottom / Left -- Three different views of the 1889 West End station.

Elberon

Bottom / Right -- Elberon station.

Deal Beach
The one-story Deal Beach station was built in 1890.

Top -- Deal Beach station.

Allenhurst
Most likely named for George Allen who laid out a small subdivision at this area. The one-story glazed-brick station was built in 1897.

Middle / Top -- A rear view of the Allenhurst station.

Middle / Middle -- A track side view of the Allenhurst station, circa 1942. Collection of James Brownback.

North Asbury Park

Middle / Bottom -- The stone North Asbury Park station.

Asbury Park
Asbury Park, also known as Ocean Grove was a prosperous beach resort town.

Bottom -- The one-story frame freight house at Asbury Park.

Page 137 -- Several different views of the Asbury Park - Ocean Grove station.

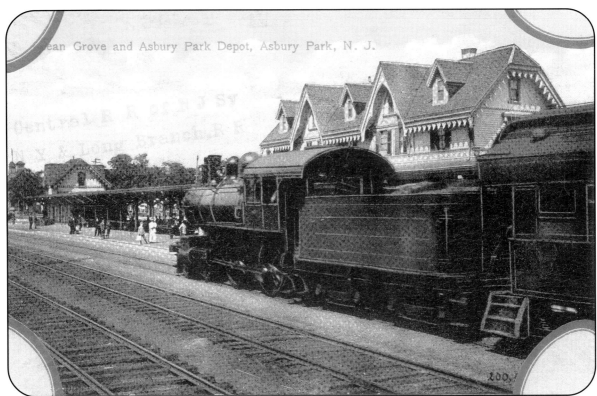

Ocean Grove and Asbury Park Depot, Asbury Park, N. J.

Bradley Beach
Top -- The Bradley Beach station was built in June, 1893.

Avon
Middle / Top -- The unique two-story frame station at Avon.

Belmar
Originally established as Ocean Beach, the name was changed to Elcho in 1889 and changed again to Belmar in 1900. A one-story story stone station served the community.

Just north of the Belmar station, the railroad crossed the Big Shark River. The railroad originally crossed the river on a long low-level wooden trestle which prevented the river from being used by commercial and military vessels. In the mid-1930s the United States War Department ordered the CNJ to replace the bridge with a drawbridge. The work was to be completed by August 30, 1937.

The construction of the new drawbridge raised the track elevation by four feet. To allow for this grade change, long approaches were constructed which forced the redesign of the 7th Street grade-crossing in Belmar. The total cost of the new 50' clear span drawbridge was $400,000 of which $40,000 was for the construction of a new interlocking and signal tower required for the proper operation of the bridge.

The bridge was finished ahead of schedule and was opened on August 16, 1937. The railroad had the temporary trestle dismantled eleven days later, allowing the river to be navigable.

Middle / Bottom -- Construction of the new Big Shark River drawbridge, circa 1937. Collection of James Brownback.

Bottom / Left -- Belmar station.

Bottom / Right -- Belmar freight house.

Como

The town of Como was laid out in 1888. A one-story stone station served the community.

Top -- Track side view of the Como station.

Middle / Top -- Rear view of the Como station.

Spring Lake

Middle / Bottom -- Rear view of the one-story brick station at Spring Lake.

Bottom / Left -- Spring Lake station, track side view.

Sea Grit

Bottom / Right -- The frame station at Sea Grit. Sea Grit was also known as Grit.

Manasquan

Top / Left -- Rear view of the Manasquan station.

Top / Right -- Manasquan station, track side view.

Pt. Pleasant

Middle / Left -- The railroad's ice house at Pt. Pleasant.

Middle / Right -- The one-story stone station at Pt. Pleasant.

Bottom -- A CNJ camelback steam locomotive sits at the Pt. Pleasant turntable, pump house and two water towers.

Matawan

For information on the Matawan station, see Chapter 18, page 126. The CNJ did maintain a turntable and an engine house at Matawan on the Freehold branch. The turntable was built in 1879 and removed in 1916. The engine house was built in 1900 and removed by 1930.

Freneau

Established in 1877 under the name of Mount Pleasant, the name was changed to Freneau in 1890. The original station was replaced in 1906 with a small one-story frame building. The station was retired in 1955 and donated to the Allaire State Park.

Top -- The Freneau station. The freight house at Freneau which can be seen to the right of the station built in 1901.

Morganville

Morganville was established as a station stop in 1877. In 1890 a one-story frame station was constructed. The station was demolished in 1953.

Middle -- The Morganville station. The freight house at Morganville which can be seen on the left of the station was built in 1903 and sold in 1951.

Wickatunk

Cooks was established in 1877. The name was changed to Wickatunk in 1879. A one-story frame station was constructed in 1900.

Bottom -- Wickatunk station. Collection of William Krug.

Bradevelt

Established in 1877 as Hillsdale, the name was changed to Bradevelt in 1884. In 1894 a one-story frame station was built. This station was replaced with CNJ wooden coach body #438 in May of 1927. The coach station was destroyed on May 22, 1951.

Marlboro

Marlboro was established as a station stop in 1877. The original station was replaced in 1892 with a one-story frame station. The station was sold in 1955. The railroad constructed a freight house in 1885.

East Freehold

Established in 1877 as a station stop. In 1897 a station was built replacing the original. The station was removed shortly after World War II.

Freehold

Freehold was established as a station stop in 1877 and a station was built. In 1884 the station was moved across the tracks to be used as an office. A new station was then constructed. The station was once again replaced in 1897 with a one-story stone building. The station was sold in 1957 and is currently being used for commercial purposes.

Top -- Bradvelt station.

Bottom -- Marlboro station and freight house.

142

CHAPTER 21
MATAWAN TO BRANCHPORT, NJ

Matawan
(See Chapters 18 and 19)

Middletown

Top -- The Middletown station was a one-story frame building.

Red Bank
(See Chapters 19 and 20)

Little Silver

Bottom -- The Little Silver station was a one-story stone building.

Branchport
(See Chapter 18)

BELFORD BRANCH, PORT MONMOUTH TO RED BANK, NJ

Port Monmouth Pier

Originally the Belford Branch originated at the Port Monmouth Pier. The pier was built in 1859-1860 and was abandoned in 1871. The pier was destroyed by an ice jam in February, 1875.

Water Tank

Established as a station stop in 1879. Lasting only four years, Water Tank was discontinued in 1883.

Hopping

Highland was established in 1860. The name was changed to Navesink in 1870 and changed again to Hopping in 1876. The first station was built in 1874 which was replaced with a one-story frame passenger shelter in 1896.

Chapel Hill

Established in 1860 as Middletown. The name was changed to Chapel Hill in 1885. The original 1874 station was replaced in 1896 with a one-story frame passenger shelter.

Top / Right -- The Chapel Hill shelter was in disrepair in 1916.

Top / Left -- Bridge #35 along the Belford Branch. The Chapel Hill passenger shelter can be seen in the background. Judging from the overgrown weeds and the deteriorate condition of the Chapel Hill shelter, this branch was not heavily used in 1916.

Hedden

Established in 1860 as Hedden's Corner, by 1862 the corner was removed from the name. This station stop was discontinued around 1870.

Red Bank

The Red Bank station was established in 1859 at Morford Place, just north of Front Street. A two-story frame station was built in 1864. The station was converted to a freight house and offices in 1879. The building was razed in 1947.

Bottom -- Red Bank station at Morford Place. Collection of William Krug.

CHAPTER 23

RED BANK TO BAYSIDE, NJ

Red Bank

The two-story frame Red Bank station was constructed on the eastbound side of the tracks in 1876. In 1902 a station was built on the westbound side.

Top / Left / Top -- The rear of the eastbound Red Bank station.

Top / Left / Bottom -- The freight house at Red Bank.

Top/ Right -- The water tower at Red Bank.

Middle / Left -- CNJ watch tower at Oakland Avenue in Red Bank.

Middle / Right -- The ash pit was part of the engine facilities at Red Bank.

Bottom -- In 1884 the railroad constructed a turntable at Red Bank. Soon afterwards a new pit was dug and the turntable was moved westward. The 1884 turntable was replaced in 1910. When diesels took over the job of the steam locomotive, the turntable was no longer needed. It was removed in 1956.

Top / Left -- The railroad maintained two water tanks at Red Bank.

Top / Right -- The coal trestle and recoaling station was built at Red Bank in 1910 and were removed in 1926. The railroad tower in the background is "RD" tower built in 1903. The tower was renamed "RG" in 1930 and renamed again in October 1972 to "BANK". The tower was closed in December 1985 and demolished in 1990.

Shrewsbury

Established in 1860 the first station, a two-story frame building was constructed in 1866. In 1876 the station was converted into a freight house and a new one-story frame station was built. The 1876 station was destroyed by fire in 1950.

Middle -- The station at Shrewsbury was built in 1876.

Bottom -- The freight house at Shrewsbury was originally the station. It was converted into a freight house in 1876, when the station in the background of the photograph was built.

Eatontown

Originally established in 1860 as Junction, the name was changed to Eatontown Junction in 1870. In 1872 the agency was moved to a new station that was constructed one quarter mile away. In 1884 the name was changed to Eatontown. The 1872 station was destroyed by fire in 1969.

Page 147 / Top -- The Eatontown station was built in 1872.

Shark River

Established as a station stop in 1861. A one-story frame combined passenger and freight station was built in 1874. A new small one-story frame station built in 1889. On January 18, 1932, Shark River was discontinued as a station stop, only to be reopened on July 18, 1932 under the name of Collingwood Park. On August 20, 1943, it was renamed again to Earle. The agency closed on March 23, 1947, and the station was retired in 1954.

Middle / Top -- Shark River station.

New Bedford

Lasting only one year as a station stop, New Bedford was established in 1862 and discontinued in 1863.

Phoenix

Established in 1892, Phoenix was discontinued in 1896.

Farmingdale

Established in 1861 with the opening of an agency in a local hotel. The railroad moved the agency into a newly constructed one-story frame station in 1889. The station was retired in 1915.

Middle / Bottom -- Farmingdale station.

Squankum

Established in 1861 as a station stop, Squankum station was built in 1874. Squankum was discontinued in 1889.

Maxim

Hendricksons was established in November, 1889. The name was changed to Maxim in 1894. A one-story frame station was built in 1891.

Bottom -- Maxim station.

Lakewood

Originally established in 1861 as Bergen Iron Works, the name was changed to Bricksburg in 1865 and to Lakewood in 1880. The first station was built near Main Street in 1865. In 1891, the Main Street station was replaced with a one-story stone station at Monmouth & Second Avenues. The station was demolished in 1953.

Mounts

Mounts was established in 1877 as a flagstop. It was discontinued around 1882.

Top / Left -- A postcard of the Lakewood station.

Top / Right -- CNJ section house near Lakewood.

South Lakewood

With the construction of a station in 1893, South Lakewood was established as a station stop. The passenger canopy was removed in 1944. A train derailment destroyed the station in 1964.

Middle -- South Lakewood station was designed with a rustic appearance.

Whites Bridge

Established as a flagstop in 1862, it was discontinued in 1869. The flagstop was reinstated in 1883 as Whites. A small one-story frame passenger shelter was built in 1888. Whites flagstop was discontinued in 1893.

Ridgeway

The flagstop at Ridgeway was established in 1862 and discontinued in 1872.

Lakehurst

Manchester was established in 1862. A two-story frame station was constructed in 1863. In May, 1897 the name was changed to Lakehurst. The station was demolished in May, 1962. The CNJ maintained engine facilities and repair shops at this location.

Bottom -- A postcard view of the Lakehurst station.

Top / Left -- In 1864 Lakehurst car shops were built. They were retired in 1935.

Top / Right -- The ash pit at Lakehurst
.

Middle -- Storehouse at Lakehurst.

Whitings

The first station was established as Whiting's Mill in 1862. The name was changed to Whitings Junction in 1870 and to Whitings in 1871 at which time a new station was built. In 1898, a joint Pennsylvania Railroad and CNJ station was built less then a mile away.

Hydraulic

Established as a station stop in 1898, it was discontinued shortly after the turn of the twentieth century.

Pasadena

Wheatland was established as a station stop around 1866. The name was changed to Pasadena in 1891. In 1884 a small one-story frame passenger shelter was constructed. The Pasadena station was retired in 1937.

Bottom / Left -- A freight house was built at Whitings in 1891, replacing one that was built in 1871.

Bottom / Right -- The passenger shelter station at Pasadena.

Bullock

Bullock was never established as a station stop. A freight house was constructed in 1885. The freight house was removed during the early 1920.

Top -- The freight house at Bullock.

Woodmansie

Established in 1862, the railroad's agency was housed in the local general store. The general store was destroyed by fire on February 4, 1892. A small one-story frame station was built in 1896. The Woodmansie station was retired in 1937.

Middle -- The Interstate Commerce Commission field inspectors take a break while inspecting the Woodmansie station.

Lebanon

Lebanon station stop only lasted for five years between 1862 and 1867.

Chatsworth

Shamong was established as a station stop in 1862. The first station was constructed in 1866. This station was replaced in 1876. The name was changed to Chatsworth in 1893. A third one-story frame station was built in 1897. The station was sold in 1952.

Pine Crest

Established in 1862 under the name of Harris Station, the name was change to Pine Crest on September 30, 1923. A station was built in 1894. Pine Crest was discontinued as a station stop in 1938.

Carranza

Established in 1900 as a flagstop under the name of Sandy Ridge, the name was changed to Carranza on July 12, 1935. It was renamed to honor Emilio Carranza, a Mexican aviator, who was killed in a crash near this location. The flagstop was discontinued in 1938.

Bottom -- Chatsworth station.

Hampton

Hampton was established as a station stop in 1862. It was discontinued around 1875. It was restored as a freight only location in 1895 as Riders Siding. In 1896 the name was changed to Ryders and a freight shelter was constructed. The freight shelter was removed in the late 1920s.

Atsion

Established as a station stop in 1862. The one-story frame station was constructed in 1870. The station was retired and sold in 1949. It was moved to a local farm where it was used by the crop pickers.

Top / Left -- Atsion station.

Parkdale

Cranberry Park was established in 1871. The name was changed to Parkdale in 1878. In 1888 a small one-story frame station was constructed. The station was retired in 1940.

Top / Right -- Parkdale station.

Chew Road

A fruit shipping platform was constructed at Chew Road in July, 1885. It was established as a flagstop in 1917. The flagstop was discontinued in 1938.

Elm

Hammonton Station was established in 1871. The name was changed to North Hammonton in 1872 and changed again to Elm in 1884. The one-story frame station was built in 1871. The station was closed in 1931 and demolished in November of 1934.

Middle -- Elm station.

Winslow Junction

Established in 1871, the first station was built in 1882. This station was replaced with a one-story fame building in 1896. The station was jointly owned between the Atlantic City Railroad and the New Jersey Southern Railroad, a CNJ subsidiary. In 1906, complete ownership of the station was transferred to the CNJ and the station was relocated. The station closed in 1975.

Bottom -- Winslow Junction station.

Page 152 / Top -- A joint ownership freight house was built at Winslow Junction in 1898. The freight house was retired in 1943.

Winslow

Winslow was established as a non-agency station stop in 1872. A passenger platform and canopy served this location. Winslow was discontinued in 1900. In 1913, Winslow was reinstated as a station stop. The stop was retired for good in 1929.

Collins Siding

Established as a flagstop 1913, Collins Siding was discontinued in 1929. A platform was constructed at this location to serve the traveling passengers.

Cedar Lake

With the construction of a combination station in 1871, Cedar Lake was established. The station was demolished in November, 1935.

Middle / Top -- The combination station at Cedar Lake.

Hebron

Hebron was established in 1891 and discontinued around 1898.

Landisville

Established in 1871, the original station was a victim of arson in October, 1911. A one-story frame combination station was quickly built to replace the original station. The station was sold in 1958 and in January, 1962, it was destroyed in a derailment.

Middle / Bottom -- The passenger / freight combination station at Landisville.

Minotola

Minotola was established in 1897. A small one-story frame passenger shelter was constructed in 1907.

Bottom -- Passenger shelter at Minotola.

Wheat Road

Established in 1871, a combination station was built in 1906. The station closed in 1938.

Main Avenue, Vineland

Established in 1871, the station was built in 1874. In 1961 the CNJ leased the station.

Vineland

Established with the construction of a station in 1871. On February 27, 1872 the station was detroyed by fire. The station was replaced that same year. In 1889 a new station, a one-story stone building, was constructed. This station was retired in 1946.

Top / Left -- The passenger / freight combination station at Wheat Road.

Top / Right -- Crossing shanty at Shilo Road near Vineland.

Middle / Left -- A postcard of the Vineland station.

Middle / Right and Bottom / Right -- The two-story frame Vineland freight house was constructed in 1889. The freight house was abandoned in 1975.

Bottom / Left -- Another view of the Vineland station.

Norma

Bradway was established in 1871. The name was changed to Norma in 1901. In 1884 a passenger shelter was built. This was replaced in 1896 with a combination station. Norma was retired in 1958.

Page 154 / Top / Left -- Norma station.

Rosenhayn

Established as a station in 1871, a one-story frame station was built soon afterwards. In 1873 a freight house was constructed. The freight house was expanded in 1891 and became a passenger / freight combination station. The station closed in 1935 and was officially retired.

Top / Right -- The original Rosenhayn station. The 1873 freight house can be seen on the right side of the photograph. Collection of William Krug.

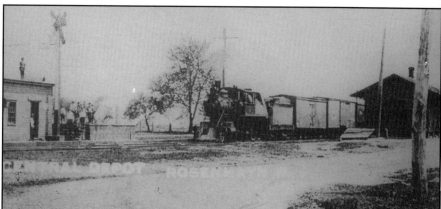

Middle -- The 1891 Rosenhayn combination station. The section on the left was the original 1873 freight house.

Garton Road

A passenger shelter was built at Garton Road in 1912, establishing it as a station stop. Garton Road was discontinued in 1929.

Bottom / Left -- Garton Road passenger shelter.

Woodruffs

Carlsburg was established in 1871. The name was changed to Woodruffs in 1872. In 1884 a passenger shelter was constructed. The shelter was replaced with a one-story frame combination station in 1908. The station closed in 1938 and was officially retired in 1941.

Bottom / Right and Page 155 / Top -- Two views of the Woodruffs Station.

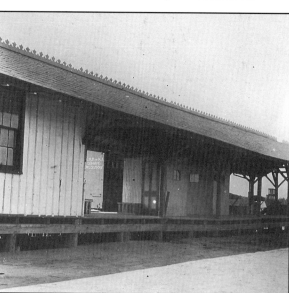

154

Bridgeton

Bridgeton was established as a station stop in 1871. A one-story frame combination station was built in 1872. A new one-story frame station was built one quarter mile away in 1884. The station was demolished in April, 1951.

A freight station of Reading Railroad design was constructed in 1884. The freight station was destroyed by fire on April 15, 1971.

Bowentown

Established in 1871, a passenger shelter was built in 1913. Bowentown was discontinued in 1923.

Middle / Top / Left -- CNJ trestle at the glass works near Bridgeton.

Middle / Top / Right -- A CNJ caboose sits on top of a coal trestle at Bridgeton.

Middle / Bottom -- CNJ section house near Bridgeton.

Sheppards Mills

A station stop was established at this location in 1871. A one-story frame combination station was built in 1891. Sheppards Mills was discontinued as a station stop in 1923.

Bottom -- Sheppards Mills station.

Greenwich

The original station at Greenwich was constructed one year after it was established as a station stop in 1871. The 1872 station was replaced in 1891 with a one-story frame station.

Greenwich Pier

Greenwich Pier was a spur off the main line of the railroad. This location was established in 1891. An oyster house and produce house were built in 1891. In 1903 a wharf was constructed. The railroad facilities were retired in 1942.

Bacons Neck

Established in 1872, a one-story frame passenger shelter was constructed at Bacons Neck in 1901. This station stop was discontinued in 1901.

155

Top / Left -- Greenwich station. Collection of William Krug.

Top / Right -- Bacons Neck passenger shelter.

Bayside

Originally established in 1872 as Bay City, the name was changed to Bayside in 1873. The railroad constructed a wharf and docks in 1872. In 1875 the original wharf was replaced. The 1875 wharf was enlarged in 1884. On November 7, 1914, the wharf was destroyed by fire. The replacement wharf was constructed in 1915. This wharf was destroyed in a severe storm on August 24, 1933.

Middle / Left -- The station at Bayside was located at the beginning of the wharf.

Middle / Right -- A view of the Bayside wharf, looking away from land.

Bottom -- The CNJ docks at Bayside.

Pine View

Germania was established as a station stop in 1877 and lasted for only one year. The station stop was reestablished around 1890 as Pine View. This location, just four and half miles away from Lakehurst was discontinued for good in 1901.

Apollonio

Established in 1887 it was discontinued in 1889.

Toms River

The first station at Toms River was constructed on the west side of the river. In 1868 this station was converted into a freight house and a new station was built on the east side of the river. The original station was destroyed in 1874 by the explosion of a gunpowder shipment.

The second station was converted into a freight house in 1900 and a new one-story stone station was constructed. The third station was sold in 1955 and was destroyed by fire in March of 1976.

Top -- The railroad trestle across the Toms River. The station can be seen on the east bank of the river.

Middle -- Toms River station.

Bottom / Left -- The freight house at Toms River was constructed in 1868 as a passenger station. This building is still standing.

Beachwood

Beachwood was established in 1915 when the Beachwood Property Owners Association constructed a one-story frame station.

Bottom / Right -- Beachwood station.

157

Pinewald

This station stop went through several name changes from its establishment in 1872. The original name was Bayville. In 1888 the name was changed to Barnegat Park and a new station was constructed by a local land development company. Around 1912 the name was changed again to Barnegat Park-Pine-wald. In June, 1921 the name was changed again to Pinewald. A large southwestern design two-story building was constructed around 1927 by the B.W. Sangor Co. to be used as their administration building and the local passenger station. This building was razed in 1974.

Top / Left -- The B.W. Sangor administration and station at Pinewald. Collection of William Krug.

Lanoka Harbor

Established in 1872 as a station stop under the name of Cedar Creek. The original station was destroyed by fire on July 14, 1888. With the construction of a one-story frame combination station in 1895, the name was changed to Lanoka. Due to a increase in passengers and freight shipments, the railroad constructed a separate station and freight house in 1900. In September, 1923 the name was changed again to Lanoka Harbor. The station was retired in 1954 and the freight house in 1938.

Top / Right -- Lanoka station.

Middle -- Lanoka freight house.

Forked River

The 1872 station was replaced with a one-story combination station in 1913. The station was retired and demolished in 1954.

Page 158 / Bottom -- Track side view of the Forked River station.

Top -- Rear view of the Forked River station.

Ostrom

Established in 1888 as a station stop, a one-story frame station was built in 1896. Ostrom was discontinued as a station stop in 1927.

Middle / Top -- By 1916 the Ostrom was converted into a passenger shelter with the removal of its windows and door.

Waretown

A station stop was established at this location in 1872. In 1900 a one-story combination station was constructed, replacing the original station. The station stop was discontinued in 1953 and the station was sold in 1955.

Middle / Bottom -- Waretown Station.

Waretown Junction

Barnegate Junction was established in 1872 as a station stop. The Barnegat Branch junctioned with the Tuckerton Railroad at this point. In 1879 the station stop was discontinued and the name was changed to Waretown Junction.

Barnegat

With the construction of a station in 1879, Barnegat was established as a station stop. This station was replaced in 1910 with a one-story frame building. The station was sold in 1949.

Being the end of the branch, the railroad maintained a turntable at this location. The turntable was constructed in 1879 and retired in 1954. An engine house was built in 1881 and it was retired in 1936.

Bottom -- The Barnegat station being used as a private residence. Collection of William Krug.

159

East Bridgeton

East Bridgeton was established as a station stop in 1882. A station was constructed in 1887. The station stop was discontinued in 1926 and the station was soon after removed. A freight house was built in 1889 and retired in 1930.

Top / Left -- CNJ produce house near East Bridgeton.

Brickville

A station stop was established at this location in 1872. It was discontinued in 1879.

Bellevue

A station stop was established at this location in 1872. It was discontinued in 1879.

Fairton

Fairton was established in 1872. The original station was rebuilt in 1880. In 1884 the station was replaced. A new one-story frame combination station was constructed in 1892. The station was closed in 1939 and officially retired in 1941.

Top / Left -- Fairton station.

Westcotts

Westcotts was established in 1872 and discontinued around the turn of the twentieth century.

North Cedarville

North Cedarville was established in 1872 and discontinued in 1901.

Cedarville

A station stop was established at this location in 1872. The original station was destroyed by fire in 1911. In 1913 the station was replaced with a one-story frame combination station. This station is still standing and was moved by the Lawrence Township Historical society in 1991.

Page 160 / Middle -- Cedarville station.

Newport

Newport was established as a station stop in 1872. The original passenger and freight stations were destroyed by fire on December 24, 1910. In 1911 a one-story combination station was constructed.

Page 160 / Bottom -- Newport station. Collection of William Krug.

Dividing Creek

In 1874, two years after Dividing Creek was established, a one-story frame station was built. This station was replaced in 1886.

Top -- Dividing Creek station.

Mauricetown

Buckshutem was established as a station stop in 1872. The name was changed to Mauricetown in 1873. The original station was replaced in 1877. In 1891 a one-story frame station was constructed. This station was removed around 1945.

Middle -- Mauricetown station. Collection of William Krug.

Centerville

Established in 1872, the station stop was discontinued in 1903.

Port Norris

Port Norris was established in 1872. A one-story frame combination station was built in 1886.

Bottom -- Port Norris station was retired in 1949.

Bivalve

Established as Long Reach in 1875, the name was changed to Bivalve in 1897. In 1880 the station was rebuilt.

Bayside View

Bayside View was established in 1875. The line from Bivalve to Bayside was abandoned in 1879.

Reading-Jersey Central Magazine

Issued Monthly by Reading Company and The Central Railroad Company of New Jersey

RESERVE YOUR COPY NOW!

Vol. 1
August
1936
No. 3

Reading - Jersey Central Magazine
Volume #1 June, 1936 to June 1937

400 page hard-bound publication
Thousands of Illustration
Unique Information
Complete Index of all 12 Issues

LIMITED TO 1000 COPIES

RESERVE YOUR COPY TODAY!

OUTER STATION PROJECT
P.O. BOX 13972
READING, PA 19612
OSPpublications@aol.com

HISTORIC JOURNEYS BY RAIL
REAIDING RAILROAD
STATIONS AND STRUCTURES OF NEW JERSEY

By Benjamin L. Bernhart

COVERING
Reading Railroad New York Line -- Trenton Junction To Bound Brook
Port Reading Railroad -- Manville To Port Reading
Atlantic City Railroad Main Line -- Camden To Atlantic City
Cape May Branch -- Winslow Junction to Cape May
Ocean City Branch -- Tuckahoe To Ocean City
  AND MORE

RESERVE YOUR COPY TODAY!

OUTER STATION PROJECT
P.O. BOX 13972
READING, PA 19612
OSPpublications@aol.com

EFFECTIVE SEPTEMBER 24, 1933
(Corrected February 1)

CENTRAL RAILROAD
OF NEW JERSEY

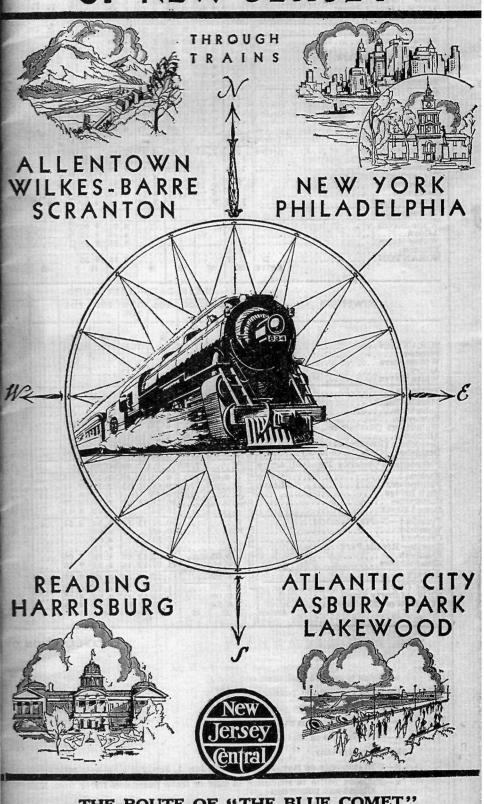

THROUGH TRAINS

ALLENTOWN
WILKES-BARRE
SCRANTON

NEW YORK
PHILADELPHIA

READING
HARRISBURG

ATLANTIC CITY
ASBURY PARK
LAKEWOOD

New Jersey Central

THE ROUTE OF "THE BLUE COMET"

T. T. 101   (40C)   10M   2-5-34   Order No. 16479